A Degree of Defiance

A Degree of Defiance

Students in
England and Europe Now

Harriet Crawley

WEIDENFELD AND NICOLSON
5 Winsley Street London W1

SBN 297 17856 3

PRINTED IN GREAT BRITAIN BY
BRISTOL TYPESETTING CO. LTD.
BARTON MANOR - ST. PHILIPS
BRISTOL

To my father
who insisted on being included in this dedication,

To my mother
who begged to be omitted,

To my two brothers at Oxford
who were sceptical of the whole undertaking.

Contents

Preface

In the last few years so much has been said and written about students that I thought it time a student should speak for herself. I am half American and have been educated in four countries. I have learnt to appreciate my generation irrespective of nationality and have described from first-hand experience the student world that I know. It is in the hope that others may come to see us more as we see ourselves that I have written this book.

A*

Aix-en-Provence

October 1966 – April 1967

MY mother, a converted American, could never see the advantage of an English boarding-school for girls. She shuddered at the thought of uniforms and hockey, high-pitched giggles and apple-pie beds. Throughout her life she has found it a great disadvantage not speaking any language other than her personal version of English. Her daughter, she decided, must speak three languages; so at the age of fourteen I left England for a gloomy convent in Neuilly, where I spent a miserable year but learnt a great deal of French. The second phase of the experiment took place in Vienna where I lived in an Austrian family and attended a state school. Pressurised tuition got me through English 'A' levels, which meant that for the six glorious months when I lived in Rome I was spared further academic pursuits and could join the academy of art.

Quite suddenly I became enthusiastic about a French university degree in political science. I planned to spend the first year of the four-year course in Aix-en-Provence, where my brother had passed an agreeable and not very arduous six months, and then move to Paris. To my delight the Faculty of Political Science in Aix accepted my application and gave me the status of a French undergraduate. It was with pride and unconcealed satisfaction that, at the end of September, I crossed the Channel in my new bright red Mini-Minor, my most treasured possession, and headed towards the Midi.

The thin blue sky that hangs over Aix turns white in the midday sun. The ground and the buildings reverberate with heat. The sharpness of the light gives the colours a new intensity. Only Monet and Cézanne transmit, in their paintings of Provence, the brightness and the stagnant heat that lies even in the purple shade of the countryside. Aix is surrounded by forests of dark green pine trees and withered olives, by yellow stone houses and brown baked earth. Five miles away, as I drove along the narrow twisting road, le Petit Cézanne, the Mont Sainte-Victoire in red and mauve rock loomed into the blue sky. The long jagged outline of the mountain fascinated Cézanne who painted it several times.

My year at Aix was dramatic from the start. On the first night all my luggage was stolen from my car. I had nothing except a black wool dress in which I had left London. Clad for a cold climate, I walked through the blazing sunshine to the Faculty of Political Science, to find that I had arrived three weeks early.

By the second evening I was installed in one of the all-female student halls of residence. Small rooms opened on to a long cold passage. At all hours of the night I could hear the sharp sound of footsteps. I felt as if I were in a mental institution; everything was white, the floor, the walls, the cupboards. For the three weeks that I lived there I did not know the luxury of hot water. In an effort to economise, the university had decided not to light the boiler until the academic year began.

Aix played an important part in Roman and Medieval French history. City walls, a church and a baptistry date from the twelfth century. Most of the houses in the old part of the town were built in the late seventeenth century. Neo-classical façades and porticos line the Cours Mirabeau, the main street of the town. Narrow streets paved with cobblestones lead to fountains and squares, and to large imposing villas that belonged to rich business men in the days when Aix, through its domestic industries, was a prosperous trading centre.

At the end of the long summer the pace of life was at its slowest. The market came and went twice a week. Its stalls cluttered the streets near the Palais de Justice, an ornate white edifice, and the old fountain square in front of the town hall.

The *pâtissiers* and the *boulangers* baked their croissants, the shopkeepers pulled down their blinds and locked their doors for three hours at lunch time. The people of Aix spent their three hours strolling along the wide pavements of the Cours Mirabeau under the shade of the chestnut trees, gazing in the shop windows at price tickets that put Paris on the level of a super-market.

Despite my premature arrival, Aix was not empty. In early October students who have failed their summer examinations sit them for the second time. At mid-day tired students emerged from their rooms, where they had been working since dawn, to sit at one of the café tables on the Cours Mirabeau and drink their *café noir*. At the Deux Garçons, my favourite café, I met several friends of my brother, among them a tall, pretty French girl, Anne, a law student. She was looking for a flat mate for the coming year. I liked her sharp, astringent manner and her sarcastic humour. Over a cup of coffee we agreed that I should move in at the end of the month. 'For the moment I must work,' she said sadly. 'But at least I only work just before the exams. They,' she went on nodding towards the figures bent over text books on the café tables, 'work from the first day of the university year to the last. Yet all they want is a small flat, a fire, a wife and their *pantoufles. C'est fou!*'

Work seemed to sap the French students of their energy. Several times I suggested taking some of my newly acquired friends for a drive. They shook their heads. 'No time,' they answered. In their few spare moments they slept, or closed their eyes in the sun.

The aura of gloom seemed quite out of keeping with the life and countryside of Provence, which I decided to explore before the term began. To the west the road to Toulon, shaded by trees, winds along the slopes of hills covered in dark green forests. In an hour and a half I found myself in Saint Tropez, a fishing village with bright coloured houses, cafés and fishing boats, unspoilt and peaceful in the absence of Brigitte Bardot and her cheetah. I drove to Cassis, a village by the sea, only half an hour from Aix. From cliffs that tower above the town, I gazed at a spectacular view of the coastline and of islands protruding from the sea like giant tortoises floating on a pond. I left the main road in the plains of Provence that stretch behind Aix, and climbed the hillsides to find heavenly villages hanging over deep valleys. Aix had everything: Roman ruins, the Mediterranean, the Spanish frontier a few hours to the south, the Alps and skiing two and a half hours to the north-east.

Ripe vineyards filled the valleys of Provence. I spent a gruelling day at the *vendanges*, picking grapes with poverty-stricken German students who had come for their holiday to the South of France and already spent their return fare home. At the end of the day my hands were chapped and swollen, my face was covered in bites from insects whose peace I had disturbed, and my back felt permanently dislocated.

Riding was a less exhausting experience. A wooden sign with an unconvincing lasso painted in black, announced an 'American Ranch'. Emaciated horses with drooping heads were tethered to a pole. 'Take your pick,' said the stable boy merrily. As I mounted, the horse nearly collapsed. 'No jumping allowed, in case of heart failure,' the stable boy shouted as we walked off towards the hills of Provence.

Eric, a small, strongly built French friend of Anne's who came from Brittany brought gaiety into the grey scene. '*J'en ai marre du travail* (I'm fed up with work),' he announced one day at the Deux Garçons, in the broad Midi accent that he adopted in Aix. '*Allons manger du paing, du vaing, et du boursaing,*' he cried; and with a flourish he swept Anne and myself and a weary friend into the open pre-war car that he had bought in Marseilles for ten pounds. In a cloud of black smoke, the engine retching and spluttering, we drove to a small village under the shadow of the Mont Sainte-Victoire. From one till five we sat and ate a delicious cheap lunch, and drowned the thought of work in the *vin de Provence*.

As the examinations approached a general depression stifled all sense of fun, and even Anne and Eric grew subdued. When at last the week arrived I went one evening with friends to hear the results announced. The white stone façade of the Faculty of Law, set against the background of cypress trees, had turned salmon pink in the sunset. As we walked through the great hall on the ground floor (in almost total darkness since the lighting was not fully installed), and climbed the wide white staircase, the scene reminded me of *The Last Judgement* in the Sistine Chapel. More than a hundred students were sitting, lying or crouching on the stairs, their strained faces turned upwards towards the door behind which the adjudicating professors were installed.

We joined Dominique, who sat chewing her nails, halfway

up the stairs. I learned that only those who had passed the written examinations, held a week earlier, could qualify for the oral examinations, the results of which Dominique and her friends were now awaiting. 'This is the last hurdle, but the most difficult,' said Dominique, 'So much depends on the mood of the professor.'

The tension on the landing was electric. Excited, breathless talk filled the corridors, half lit by the light from the examination room. For two hours we sat in semi-darkness. Nervous hands waved cigarettes that shone like glow-worms in the dim light. A girl sat by herself in a corner, crying with her head in her hands. As I watched the anxious twitching faces I realised that each one of these students cared desperately about his or her examinations. The drone of conversation stopped suddenly as a professor came down the stairs, but started up once again as he shook his head and told students that the final decision had not been reached. It was eight o'clock but no one left for dinner. Sporadic conversation had lost the false tone of gaiety that it held earlier. A voice behind me murmured, ' I shall die if I have to repeat the year.'

The sound of footsteps silenced all talk. From the second floor the professors walked slowly down the stairs into the examination room. One held a list in his hand. The students sitting on the stairs rose together in a wave, and crowded round the glass door. In a loud voice the long-awaited list of names was read out. Dominique heard her name and hugged me and her friend, and with an elated smile passed into the examination room to hear her exact result. I could tell at once those whose names had not been mentioned from their dejected and despairing faces. The others hugged each other and danced and shouted along the corridors. ' Well done' and 'Bad luck' echoed along the walls. Boys comforted girls in tears, girls took their despondent friends by the arm, and joined the mass exodus down the stairs through the dark hall into the cold air. Everyone walked or ran towards the centre of Aix, longing to forget the cold room and the professors. 'Now for a huge dinner and a lot of wine,' Dominique cried and I followed willingly.

I was enchanted by the beauty of my surroundings and the first weeks passed quickly. In the third week in October I moved into Anne's lodgings. 'I have found one of the best flats in Aix,' she told me one day. 'It is the Ritz compared with what I lived in last year.' At Number Three, rue Maréchal Foch, a charming street in the heart of the old town, she pushed open a narrow door and I followed her along a dark corridor, past dustbins and empty boxes, up five flights of stairs. Paint was peeling from the yellow walls. Washing hung from open windows into the narrow courtyard around which the flats had been built. Broken furniture and mattresses with protruding springs cluttered the landings. On the fourth landing outside a low wooden door that led into a flat we nearly tripped over a sleeping body wrapped in newspaper. 'He's the son, and his mother won't let him in until he gets a job,' said Anne in a bored disinterested voice. We reached the fifth floor, panting. Anne pushed open the narrow door and proudly showed me into our ' *appartement* '.

It was a one-room attic, divided into two rooms by a paper-thin wall and a glass door. The larger room served as my bedroom, the work room, sitting-room and kitchen. We had a two-ring gas stove and a cold water tap above a shallow sink. Behind a plastic curtain, a shower and a basin constituted our bathroom. Outside on the landing we shared the squat lavatory with the other occupants of the floor. The light repeatedly failed in the lavatory and so we bought a supply of candles. This almost proved disastrous because one day Anne forgot to blow the candle out. We were peacefully drinking coffee in our flat when we noticed smoke curling up from under the door. With a scream Anne jumped up and rushed to the lavatory. The flame had caught the piles of dried wood and newspapers heaped on a shelf above the pan, and now six-foot flames were leaping to the skylight. In a panic of efficiency Anne found a bucket, and I took the plastic washing bowl. Through the thick smoke we flew in and out of the flat carrying water that we threw over the raging flames. With deep relief we watched them reduced to smoking cinders. Then as we leaned exhausted against the wall, another crisis loomed. From the flat opposite we heard a woman shriek furiously, 'Are you trying to drown us all?' The uneven floor of the passage sloped towards her flat and the water had joined in a neat stream and was flowing along the landing under her door. The woman, looking in disgust at her damp slippers, showed no interest in the hissing smoke that poured from the lavatory – which was as much hers as ours. 'We have almost been burned alive and all she can think about are her *pantoufles, mon Dieu*,' Anne whispered, and stifling our hysterics we brought out mops and rags and sopped up the black water.

Our flat had a Van Gogh character, with its sloping ceiling, broken furniture and bare walls. We both felt so proud of our independence and new ownership status that we did not give the squalor a thought. '*C'est un appartement merveilleux*,' Anne announced as she pinned up our names outside the door. 'Last year we lived in a flat with only one small window, and no hot water. *C'est le vrai luxe.*'

Dust rises, so we were to learn, but it was easy to overlook the discomfort as the bright autumn light lit up the low rooms. From the wide window above my bed I looked out on to the red roof tops, the chestnut trees and the church spires of Aix, to the range of green hills behind the town. Directly below us I could see the small square in front of the town hall. Flower stalls clustered around an eighteenth-century fountain. A seventeenth-century clock tower, arched over the road, chimed the hours of the day. Through the trees I could see the market square, where each morning food stalls arrived from the countryside. It was either the shout of a fish-wife, or the bells from the clock tower, or the noise of the market shoppers, or the blast from a band out to meet the mayor, or the sweet smell of one of Aix's thirty-seven *pâtisseries* which stood directly beneath us, that woke us in the morning.

Anne's parents lived in Marseilles. Though their flat was in the residential part of the city and always meticulously neat and extremely comfortable, she was oblivious to the dirt of our garret. She loved Aix, where she spent the week, and never grew tired of, or indifferent to, the beauty of the town and of Provence. Although not at all religious, Anne was basically moral and had strong views on most subjects. She held unyieldingly that *jeunes filles* should be virgins when they marry and set great store by outward appearances, particularly manners. Anne felt that girls should not speak to strangers. At the university restaurant, where we ate each night, she never spoke to people she did not know. Trivial details prejudiced her. I watched a promising flirtation end suddenly when the boy committed a grave fault in French etiquette: he cut his salad with his knife. Anne frowned with

17

disappointment. I could see her illusions were shattered.

Her sense of right and wrong made her dogmatic to many of her friends, yet I discovered an inexplicable paradox in her nature. While normally so upright and *bourgeoise,* she had not the slightest qualm in following the general trend of students and pinching freely from the university restaurant and small cafés. She produced, as if by magic, knives and forks, ashtrays and napkins, and anything else we needed. 'I found these,' she would announce, her eyes laughing.

Anne's sarcasm offended girls and attracted boys. While we were sitting at the Deux Garçons together, a girl came up and asked if she might join us. Anne knew her slightly and did not like her. '*Je peux m'asseoir?*' asked the girl. '*Si ça peut faire plaisir,*' came Anne's uncompromising reply.

Anne thought French girls 'catty' and knew very few in Aix. 'They tear each other's eyes out where boys are concerned. Loyalty is thrown to the winds.' On the other hand she was tolerant towards young men. With great discretion she asked me one day about a rather slimy youth with whom I had been to the cinema. I gave her a blunt, unattractive picture of the French boy. With relief she said, '*Alors, il ne faut pas le considérer comme le beau-frère du moment.*' (Good, I needn't consider him as your current boy-friend.)

Most of her friends were foreigners. '*Les Français sont mortels,*' (The French are deadly), she told me once. Her father, a Jew, had spent the last two years of the war in a concentration camp. He was a saintly man and, though he suffered terribly at the hands of the Gestapo, he never infused anti-German feeling into his children. For three years Anne had had German boy-friends and her father showed them kindness and hospitality.

Throughout the year I met no other girl whom I liked as much as Anne. For the first few weeks that we shared a flat another exceptional individual joined us, Eric. He had failed his final examination and had nowhere to sleep. Anne offered him a camp bed on the floor and for over a month he stayed as our guest. Other friends of his roamed in and out, some sleeping on chairs and cushions. In the morning we crept out of bed, uncertain whom we might find on the floor.

At first Eric called me *Ma grande,* and Anne, *Ma cocotte.*
Eric revelled in vulgarity. His table manners were as atrocious
as mine. He drank yoghourts to which Anne objected furiously,
saying he was debasing our standards of civilisation. His jokes
were obscene but funny. In the morning he left his clothes
strewn all over the flat, while his books sat on chairs and tables
adding to the chaos.

Eric supported himself by working as an assistant teacher
during most of the day. In his free time he studied. When he
discovered that he had failed his finals he went to see his professor who did not realise that he had taken his third and fourth
year examinations at the same time in an attempt to finish early.
'If only you had told me before,' he said, much to Eric's
fury.

On hot afternoons we drove around in Eric's open car. Anne
and I sat in the back while Eric flirted with his naïve
Swedish girl-friend. 'She needs to be cultivated,' he told us with
a wink. From the back seat we watched out for the police as
Eric made strictly forbidden U turns on the Cours Mirabeau,
ignoring the yellow line.

On 21 October the university burst into life. A surfeit of
cars blocked the Cours Mirabeau and the pavements swarmed
with students. Aix is the university for Marseilles in all subjects
except mathematics and science. Each morning ten thousand
students commuted from Marseilles; another ten thousand
spent the week in Aix and went home to Marseilles at the week-
end. Over two thousand foreigners poured into the city, many
on university-exchange programmes.

The university campus is on the outskirts of the town. The
halls of residence overlook the new faculties of Law and Letters.
More students live off the campus than on it. Off the campus
you might be installed in a small dark room, with half a window, a wooden floor and thin walls, with a leaking roof that
your landlady refuses to repair and a squat lavatory three floors
below you. On the campus you are given a small bare room,
with a desk that takes up half the floor-space (the university likes
to keep the furniture in perspective) and an army camp bed in
the corner. When the hot water is turned on the rooms can be
made quite comfortable for those who can stand collective living,

collective eating and collective washing.

Some of my foreign friends paid exorbitant sums to stay with a French family. Others, who valued their independence, shared a villa or took a room in one of the modern blocks of flats, if they could afford the high rent. Whether you lived in the *cité universitaire* or a garret, in the evening all students joined the stream towards one of the university restaurants. The most amusing, the Gazelles, where Anne and I ate each evening, was part of the main university campus. Though every one of the university restaurants could seat two thousand, queues of two hundred people assembled every evening outside the door.

My first lesson in student life was to lose all respect for queues. In France a queue is not a hall-mark of civilisation as it is in England. The French say good luck to anyone who can worm his way to the front. Every evening adventurous boys scaled walls, walked along narrow ledges, jumped over high wire netting, to avoid the long wait. Those too inert to make the effort whiled away the time examining the advertisements on the billboards. An unusual notice, which caused much laughter, read – 'Please stick any hairs found in soup, or slugs in salad, to this piece of paper.' Sellotape attached one strand of hair to a white sheet of paper. The question asked was, 'Who will stick up the first slug?' While I was at Aix none appeared.

The food, which cost only two shillings, was good by English standards and, more important, plentiful. I gave up the first course, soup, after a few days because it was an impractical dish. After the soup you had to eat two other courses on the same plate and I was too fond of the lettuce that was served with every meal to see it smeared with soup remains. Yoghourt presented other problems. With no small spoons you had the choice between the end of your knife or the handle of the soup spoon. Eric of course drank it, sucking the thick curdled milk noisily through his teeth.

I shall never forget the first meal I ate at the Gazelles. I had a piece of dark brown meat on the end of my fork ('*c'est du cheval*' – 'It's horse,' Anne had warned me), and was transferring it to my mouth when a hand shot through the gap made by my arm, leaving me in suspended animation, picked up the salt cellar and withdrew. I turned in amazement to the young man next to me. He neither looked at me nor said a word but sat on the edge of his chair, vigorously stirring his mashed potatoes into which he plunged lettuce leaves. He mopped up his plate with bread, and then started to mop drops of gravy on the table. Watching him I realised that from the moment a student joined the queue to the moment he left the dining hall his meal was a struggle for survival.

The Deux Garçons seemed civilised after the Gazelles. By eight o'clock in the evening all the chairs were taken and the air smelt of delicious black coffee. The cafés on the Cours Mirabeau were the centre of student life. For most of the year tables and chairs stood on the wide pavement shaded by the plane trees. At the cafés you met your friends, drank *citron pressé* in summer and hot chocolate in winter, ate breakfast, wrote letters, or just sat in the sun and argued with anyone who had the time to argue back. On hot summer days students who could not stand the claustrophobic atmosphere of their small rooms brought their work to the cafés.

Most of the famous cafés on the Cours Mirabeau have a long-standing political tradition and attract a specific type of student. I visited all the cafés in turn and in each felt I was watching one act of a play about Aix. Near the Rond Point the cafés tended to be left wing. The Mondiale, small and drab, was the meeting place for communist students. Sullen, thin boys and girls sat at the tables, dirty and in ragged jeans. Farther up the Cours, the Longchamps would have been the choice of the Fabian Society. The intellectuals of Aix, wearing thick-rimmed glasses and carrying *Le Monde*, sat drinking cups of black coffee, surrounded by photographs of jockeys and horses at the famous race track. Although the chief waiter, a charming man with a thin black moustache, had never been to university, he had educated himself and was an authority on German philosophy. 'In the old days,' he sighed, 'when Aix was a small university, I spent many hours discussing philosophy with students. Now everyone is in a hurry.' However, late at night, I often went to the Longchamps to play bridge in the back room and found Jean deep in conversation with young Frenchmen. The room seldom resounded with laughter. It was full of students discussing how to put the world to rights.

At the Grillon, twenty yards down the street, the moderate conservatives and socialists met, united by an intense dislike of de Gaulle. Few students in Aix supported their President. Many had ties with North Africa and the *Pieds Noirs* – the French citizens of Algeria and Morocco – and bitterly resented '*la trahison de de Gaulle.*' The Grillon bubbled with life and laughter. It served the best coffee, entertained the most amusing students, the '*Yé Yés*' of Aix, in their tight bell-bottom trousers, *minipulls* (minisweaters), curling sideboards and hair just long enough to scandalise the conservative but money-conscious shop-keepers.

Wholly unsophisticated, the Grillon was the *Action Café*, the 'with it' joint frequented by Iona, the Brazilian student expelled from his country for political propaganda against the government; by Ionel, the vociferous Hungarian; by the *Pieds Noirs*; and the beatniks and the misfits of Aix.

Next to the Grillon, the Deux Garçons, owned by the French National Trust, was the most famous café in Aix. The green and gold canopy, the ornate lamps that were reflected by walls lined with mirrors, the wood carvings above the doors, the large rooms and the vast section of pavement occupied by the green tables and chairs, gave the Deux Garçons an air of distinction. Politically it was right wing. The 'smoothies' of Aix in their smart red sports cars, who regarded university as an agreeable pastime, brought to its doors their chic girl-friends who wore black trousers, tight sweaters and black berets, or lace stockings and plain dresses. The most sophisticated and self-confident girls were the daughters of the old Aixois families, who did not mix with the ordinary students but kept closely to their own set. Their smart decorum was sometimes disturbed by the Bohemians, noisy groups of boys and girls who used to screech to a stop in front of the café in their black Mini-Coopers decorated with ticker tape and giant white squares, shriek hello to their friends, give each other dramatic kisses on the cheek (very *avant-garde* in Aix, where the custom among students is to shake hands), and bring a general sigh of relief when they left.

Anne liked the Deux Garçons because of its air of respectability. In truth the subdued conversation and correct appearance served as a cover for the most intensive *dragueurs* of the town. (*Draguer* is an untranslatable word roughly meaning 'to vet the opposite sex.') At the Deux Garçons, whenever a pretty girl came through the doors or sat outside at a table, fifty pairs of male eyes surreptitiously watched her every move while she pretended not to notice.

Few students passed by both the Grillon and the Deux Garçons to sit at the Royal, the last café on that side of the Cours. With the Royal the political wheel reached its full circle, for it was the home of the fascists and oligarchists. They are a dying race, and the café was almost always deserted.

I was excited as I walked towards the amphitheatre to hear my first lecture. From Anne and Eric I had formed a general impression of the French university system. To obtain a *licence,* the equivalent of a BA, students had to gain a certain number of certificates by passing annual written and oral examinations. The certificates were based on series of lectures held throughout the year. If anyone failed they could retake the examinations as often as they liked until they passed. Students had little choice in subject mater. In most faculties the syllabus was meticulously planned. Anne pointed out that seminars were gaining increasing importance and for most students were obligatory. Officially, lectures were also obligatory, but no attendance sheets were kept.

Although I arrived early, when I walked into the amphitheatre I was surprised to find all the seats taken. Over three hundred students filled the long narrow benches and rested their arms on the straight planks of wood that served as writing shelves. I joined the overflow sitting in the gangway. The professor arrived, a few pairs of hands applauded weakly, and the lecture on constitutional law began. As the first word came over the loud-speakers, three hundred pens started scratching and did not stop until the last word of the lecture had been uttered. I could not believe my eyes. The students were not taking notes, they were taking dictation, scribbling at a speed that left no time for thought. At the end of the lecture I asked a student why he took down every word. ' You must,' he answered, ' if you don't take down everything you may not know the answer to a precise question in the oral examination, and you will fail. *C'est très simple.*'

' But how can you absorb what the professor is saying?'

' You can't at the time. But once you have everything written down you can read it later.'

' But why do you have to know every single detail?'

'Because our examinations are based almost entirely on lectures given by the professors. In the oral examinations these notes are the official sources of knowledge. Although for the written examination the professor gives us the names of a few recommended books, if you learn the lectures by heart you needn't read them.'

'Learn the lectures by heart! But what if you do not agree with your professor?'

The student looked at me in amazement. 'Of course you agree with the professor. How can you have another opinion if you do not know anything? Anyway the lectures are not the personal opinion of the professor. They are quite unbiased.'

I recalled these words as I heard the opening sentence of my second lecture. 'Montesquieu is superior to Locke for the three following reasons . . . ' and the professor spelled them out. Indignantly I put down my pen, but all around me, with chauvinistic smiles of satisfaction, students took down every golden syllable.

Anne told me that in her first year of law she had followed half of the prescribed lectures. The others she had learned by heart from the photostat copies issued each year by a student organisation. Anne handed me a copy of the course in constitutional law. 'The professors read off the same lectures year after year. That copy is pre-war, but still valid today,' she added sarcastically. I looked at the lecture for the following day, and then for the following weeks. It was like glancing through the list of prescribed Bible texts to be read in church each Sunday. I felt very depressed at such an impersonal approach to learning. I noticed that many students simply took their photostat copies to the lectures, and followed the texts with their pens, making minor alterations whenever the professor deviated from last year's version.

'What an idiotic way to learn,' I exploded to Anne one evening. But she had long ago resigned herself to the university system. 'I shall get out of it what I can,' she said philosophically.

I asked Monsieur Fabre, an eminent professor of law, *Doyen* of the Faculty of Political Science and founder of the University of Madagascar, what value he placed on the individual thoughts of his students.

'While they are undergraduates, absolutely none,' he answered bluntly. 'Our aim is to train young minds to think logically. We present them with carefully prepared arguments which we expect them to learn by heart and reproduce in their examinations. Thus, by memorising illustrations of logical thought, they learn to apply logic to fresh situations, to think coherently. The information we give in lectures is material digested from an infinite number of sources. In learning it by heart a student develops his powers of reason and above all acquires knowledge. We believe that before the individual opinion can be seriously considered, a student must have the basic knowledge to back up his arguments. We therefore insist that students learn what we teach. As this takes up most of the academic year, students do not have time for original research and we, the professors, would not have the time to correct their work if they did. In my opinion, it is much more important to give students the raw materials with which to advance than to let them play with thoughts. What is the point of asking young people who have just left school for their opinions on subjects about which they know so little?'

The lack of individual attention and the resignation of French students towards the rigid university system made a deep impression on me. I realised though, that the attitude of the professors was not new to the students at Aix, since education in French *lycées* is based on the same principle. I recalled the year I had spent at a French convent school in Neuilly. The teachers showed not the slightest interest in the girls as individuals. 'Learn the page by heart,' was all that we heard. Whether one was studying history or mathematics the homework was memorising. In my class, the *troisième*, the fourth year before the final school examinations, the history teacher had the formidable task of instructing her pupils in three hundred years of history, in order to leave uncluttered for the following year the glorious reign of Napoleon. Our literature, like our history, consisted of the names of writers, their dates and their principal works, to be learned by heart. We never had time to read their books, but none of my classmates seemed to think it necessary. Their attitude was that whatever the teacher told them about the book must be right.

At the lectures in Aix, I felt I was once more at school. The meekness of my fellow undergraduates puzzled me. The French are by nature alert and critical and in Aix the students were not stupid. They were the heirs of a still lively revolutionary tradition which frequently emerged in their arguments about de Gaulle. Yet like sheep before the sheep-dog they tamely allowed their minds to be drilled and penned by their instructors.

I came to the conclusion that it was all due to fear, fear of failing an examination. Nothing is more highly revered in France than academic achievement. To belittle the intelligence of a French student is the most wounding of insults. At my school, one day, a severe teacher told a girl that the only job she was fit to do was that of a charwoman. The girl broke into hysterics.

Children are taught by their parents that scholastic failure is the deadliest of sins. Teachers endorse this view, with the result that by fair means or foul French children are determined to pass. Highly organised cheating was a constant feature at my school. Pupils who could not stand the strain pleaded illness. My room-mate, a boarder like myself, ate a bar of soap the night before the examination and in the morning was too sick to get up. 'I know I would fail and I am too frightened to face my parents,' she told me in tears.

Anne told me of the nation-wide cheating the year that she took her finals. 'The week before the *bachot*, our teacher rang each one of us up and told us to come to the school on Saturday afternoon. She had got hold of the examination papers – we never knew how – and we went over them with her. Four days later, wonderfully prepared, we sat the examination.' None of Anne's class hesitated to take advantage of the illicit lesson. To pass their *bachot* was all-important. The cheating did not pay, however, as two weeks later the papers were annulled when the Ministry of Education realised that there had been a massive leak. New examinations were then held.

At Aix I began to realise that to most French students university is nothing more than a continuation of school. Even during seminars, when students have the chance to express themselves, they are so unused to saying what they think that the professor is often forced to take over the class and deliver a lecture. Few professors have the time to conduct their own seminars and they give this task to their assistants, young graduates working

26

for a doctorate. Seminars have not the slightest bearing on the university examinations. They are simply extra classes in which an attempt is made to give each student individual attention. In theory they should consist of small groups, but in many faculties seminars are obligatory and there are so many students that discussion is impossible. In my faculty of political science I counted only fourteen names, other than my own, on the list and my hopes for an interesting seminar rose.

The first seminar of the year began at nine o'clock on a Wednesday morning. The Faculty of Political Science was on the same road as our flat, in one of the original university buildings. In the back two rows of the attic classroom all fourteen students sat side by side, leaving the front six rows of chairs empty. The assistant professor looked nervous and fumbled with his spectacles. He announced what books we were expected to read in the next term and then tried to open a discussion. His questions met with complete silence. Each face seemed to say, ' Please just do not ask me.' The girl beside me whispered to her friend, ' Why doesn't he just give us something to write down?' By singling out students and forcing them to talk the assistant at least heard a voice other than his own. But not one student spoke of his own free will.

' If you think this class is dull you should come to some of the others,' laughed the assistant when I spoke to him afterwards. 'I could bang my head against the wall and no one would stir.' He explained that the idea of free expression was so foreign to first year students that it took at least one year and often two for them to enter freely into a class discussion. 'They never speak because they are afraid of being wrong.'

Eric agreed with what he said. ' We are taught to accept passively what we are told, and though we do not accept all that we hear, we do not learn how to develop and express our dissent. For two years I was incapable of arguing.'

By February of the new year my seminar was no longer a lesson in which students could voice their opinions. The assistant had found so little response that he turned to didactic school methods. At the end of a prepared talk by one of the students, instead of calling for a free discussion the young assistant dismissed the speech with a few brief comments and then read out his own thoughts on the subject which were taken down word for word by the rest of the class. Model essays and model speeches had become the meat of the seminar. Controversy was still-born. One day the subject for discussion was 'The Qualities of all Great Men'. The assistant solemnly read out a list: 'Inspiration, Intelligence, Imagination, Ambition.' Not a murmur rose from the class. Twelve pens scratched away in complete silence. 'They will not think,' the assistant said afterwards in desperation.

Nor will they read. One day I was sitting in the Deux Garçons when a friend came to me with a piece of paper in his hand. 'I must write a commentary on this extract from Proust,' he said, laying the printed sheet on the table. It was a famous passage from *Un amour de Swann*. 'Have you read the book?' he asked. I nodded, 'Ah,' he said with relief, and sat down. 'You are the first person I have met who knows the book. I do not understand what this passage is about. Can you tell me something about the characters?'

I was so intrigued by this approach to literature that I asked him about his studies. His main subject was German and he took French as his second language. The extract from Proust had been allotted to him by the assistant in a seminar. No suggestion had been made that he should read the book. He was just to comment on the style and content of the text, although anyone who had not read the book must find it incomprehensible. So I spent an hour telling him all I could remember about *Un amour de Swann*, one of my favourite books. He listened attentively and at the end of our conversation paid me a charming compliment. He might read the book after all, he said.

I could have understood this French attitude to education if the method had been successful, but in every faculty at least fifty per cent of the students failed their exams, and often the percentage was higher. Many students fail because they do not work, but even my most intelligent friends faced their examinations with uncertainty because they felt that they were not being tested on their capacity to think but on their ability to reproduce facts. Yet although students all over France complained bitterly about the university system, I was amazed that they did nothing to change it. In England and Italy if students found their lectures uninteresting they stayed away and got the information from books. In France they filed into the amphitheatres however bored they might be with the lecturer. Only once did I see some students rebel. I was sitting with Anne and a group of her friends at the back of the largest amphitheatre listening to a lecture on criminal law. The professor was wallowing in his own eloquence, reading the lecture that he had written in the first term of his professorship many years ago. He repeated what he thought a significant phrase twice. A friend of Anne's shouted, ' We are not in the kindergarten. We heard the first time.' Throughout the lecture, from the back of the hall there were cries, 'This is too dull,' 'This information is not worth taking down.' In the middle of the lecture Anne's friends rose to their feet and, causing consternation among the students, left the hall shouting to each other, 'Hurry or we shall miss the film.' No one else followed their example.

Some French professors deplore their own system. The head of the History Faculty at Toulouse, Professor Wolfe, admitted that his students saw no interconnecting ideas in history, which they regarded as names and facts, politics and philosophy. ' They fail to see that each historical event is the result of a political opinion. Of course our students are dull. Throughout their schooldays they are crushed. It takes them at least the first two years of university to emerge as individuals. But many good brains never make the effort.'

Perhaps the *Plan Fouchet*, a radical reform of university education which de Gaulle's old colleague in the Resistance has introduced, will change French universities. The main problem is too many students and too few professors. Fouchet has introduced a watertight system of selection. He has divided higher education into three ' cycles '. The first consists of a two-year programme culminating in a difficult examination. Students can fail only once. Those who do so may prepare for a revised *licence* or apply to an Institute of Technology. Those who pass begin the second cycle, a one-year programme that leads to the final examination and new equivalent of the British BA, the *Maîtrise*. Post-graduate research and advanced teacher-training make up the third cycle. The rigidity and crushing selection of the plan are widely attacked, though it will, if it survives, undoubtedly reduce the number of students.

Professor Wolfe hopes that, as universities become less

crowded, students will have more contact with their professors. 'Our universities must become more personal,' he emphasised. Many of my friends in Aix longed to discuss their subject with their professors, men of great learning, instead of with the assistants who were only a few years older than themselves. In time perhaps, as a result of the *Plan Fouchet*, the students in France may, as a visiting German professor suggested, become the subjects and not the objects of the university.

Even in December the sun shone in Aix and dappled the Cours Mirabeau with its pale light. I was learning to be more tolerant. 'Take the trouble to get to know people,' Eric advised. I was immensely fond of him. He had worked his way through university without a word of complaint. Anne also was unfailingly kind; several times I had dined with her parents in Marseilles. In Aix she took me to her Law classes where I met a new world of friends.

The Cours Mirabeau was almost deserted; I was walking in the late afternoon with Jean, a third-year Law student, who gazed out bemused from behind his round spectacles while he philosophised. He stopped in front of a plane tree. 'It doesn't exist. Work it out for yourself,' he remarked urbanely. I did, and found that he was right. We moved on to a café where we met Patrick whom I had seen the week before in the student revue. That day, on the Fête des Rachimbourgs, Aix University had burst into life. Hundreds of people had clamoured to hear the traditional Latin speeches outside the town hall; bangers exploded, balloons floated into the cold air. In the municipal theatre Law professors, among them Fabre, had arrived amid cat-calls and boos to see themselves caricatured in satirical sketches. Jean compèred, Patrick acted, and I applauded wildly.

'Why be afraid of old men, *c'est à nous l'avenir*,' Patrick remarked as he sipped the *bouillabaisse* soup. We were dining in a small restaurant in Marseilles overlooking the harbour. Lights flickered on the restless water and the air smelled of salt. 'You English think we are anti-social,' Jean said petulantly, 'but after all, *on n'est pas obligé d'aimer tout le monde*!' 'The English make excellent friends because they are such rotten relations,' Patrick intervened. 'My relations are never out of the house. My mother centres her life around our boring, prying *famille*,' Jean moaned. We talked late. I felt a sense of communication that was new and exciting; already my criticisms of Aix were melting.

As I took part in the life in Aix I was struck by the wide knowledge of the older French students and by their ability to argue succinctly. At a meeting of the Young Europeans, a Philosophy student who had just talked on German industrial relations explained, 'For all its faults our educational system does have one advantage: it teaches us to talk, and talk, and talk. Just look at de Gaulle . . . So many words to say so little!' An argument followed, and everyone was happy.

Later I went to a discussion on art at the house of a young painter. 'What is this picture?' I asked a man who was plucking a mandolin. 'A stone,' he answered. The canvas was covered with brown paint and grey splodges. 'A stone,' he reiterated, 'magnified.' Anne and Jean arrived and we talked about God and death and Harold Pinter until five in the morning. I had been too critical about Aix, I thought to myself. As Jean had said to me, ' The only truth about a university that I have learnt is that you get out of it what you put in.'

Nevertheless I longed to leave Aix University, not because of the work, since the subject-matter was fascinating, nor because of the professors who were highly cultivated and intelligent men, but because of the system that I had grown to hate. Anxiously I waited for a reply to my application to King's College, London University, which might give me an alternative to the grim prospect of four years of *Sciences Politiques*. I realised that I lacked the perseverance to continue the course and genuinely admired my French class-mates for their application although I knew that they had little choice.

A letter came from King's College calling me for an interview and I left for London overjoyed. When I returned in the New Year my academic future was secure and my time my own. I threw off my depression, determined to make the most of the months that remained to me in Provence, and even to mingle with the foreigners and the *fous Anglais* whom I had so studiously avoided. The institute for foreigners received with open arms the flower of English youth, fresh from the playing fields of Eton and other eminent public schools. After their monastic life,

31

and free for the first time from parental and scholastic super-vision, neither work nor sport were foremost in their minds. They discovered sex and were obsessed by it.

Few English boys made any effort to learn French, nor were they able to make friends among the French students. They kept together, convinced that the French resented the presence of foreigners. Known as the English 'colony', they collected around a long table at the Deux Garçons at least once a day and read William Hickey to each other referring nostalgically to life at home. Their energy, however, astounded Aix. Every week an English car left for Italy, for northern France, for Germany or Spain, even for North Africa. Those who stayed in Aix explored the Côte d'Azur, and ski'd in the Basses Alpes. Their laughter resounded along the Cours Mirabeau. The police had their hands full coping with their exuberant celebrations on the even-ing of November the fifth. Several of the English bathed in the fountains while others decorated the statues with flowers and old clothes. On one of the last evenings of the winter term, to com-memorate a friend's departure, Simon Crocker, the wit of the colony, planned to throw soap suds into the gushing waters of the fountain. We all envisaged a huge white foamy cloud settling lightly on the Rond Point. Alas, the police, warned of the pro-ject, turned off the water and Simon went home with the suds in his pocket.

I had one American friend who lived on five plates of chips a day. Most Americans segregated themselves from the English and French students. Occasionally the more eccentric walked down the Cours Mirabeau in Red Indian clothes. They intro-duced the English to pot. Marijuana was pushed by a terrify-ing character, Frank, six and a half feet tall, cross-eyed, recently let out of a remand home. Few of my friends were under the illusion that marijuana gave them greater insight into life. It gave them a cheap kick and no hangover.

In my new spirit of release I drove all over the Alpes Mari-times, the Côte d'Azur, the Basses Alpes. Anne and Eric some-times joined me on my expeditions to the Roman towns of Pro-vence. Less often could I persuade them to come skiing or to spend a week-end in Saint Tropez, since it took up so much of their time. For my last few months in Aix I attended only the lectures that I liked. While I was enjoying the warm spring and the beauty of Provence, the shadow of examinations had already fallen over French student life.

French boys had found their steady girl friends, many had chosen their wives. Hand in hand the couples walked through the university buildings, made love at the back of the cinemas, sipped coffee together at an intimate café table, took notes side by side in the lecture halls. It was love *en famille* at the student halls of residence. In the boys' buildings the guard spent most of his time watching television and did not notice the shadows that passed under his window late at night. Each *copain* had his *copine* and Aix seemed full of newly-weds. 'They are already dreaming of a fire-side, warm slippers and screaming babies,' said Anne in despair.

The *copine* gave her *copain* moral support and vice versa as the examination ordeal approached. Conversation was magnetically drawn to the subject of work. Stencilled copies were already in demand for students to check whether they had missed anything in their notes. Heads bowed and faces grew glum at the thought of the coming strain. As the cloud of depression closed in on Aix foreigners felt ill at ease. They prolonged their trips abroad, cut short their stay. I spent several nights writing poetry which I tore up as I watched dawn throw its pink light over the roofs of the town.

Fortunately, while wallowing in this self-conscious mood, I met Erner, an Icelander of twenty-four who was taking a graduate course in philosophy. He spent each Christmas in a monastery, though he had no intention of becoming a monk. At Aix he seldom came out of his room, where he sat day and night writing his novel. He kept the window shut. 'Fresh air hurts my lungs,' he told me. One evening he announced that he was leaving for Paris. 'I must reach the heart of French culture, I cannot find it here,' he said. He offered me the sixth place in a four-seater car, leaving the following evening, arriving in Paris for breakfast. I gladly accepted.

That night I ate an enormous dinner at the Rotonde with Simon and my American friend Glenn. They both wore dinner jackets. When I arrived in an evening dress I found them sitting at a table by the window. They got up and formally presented me with a rose. French students in their day clothes were sitting at the other tables and on high stools by the bar. They had seen us so often in dirty sweaters and jeans, that now they sadly shook their heads. '*Comment faire le marché commun avec ceux-là,*' they muttered. Perhaps they were right.

2

Paris

January 1967

A TALL thin man in his early twenties leant on the bridge that joins the Ile Saint-Louis to the Left Bank. His hair was long and he wore jeans and a sheepskin jacket. On the pavement in front of him was written in white chalk, 'I can't paint but I am hungry.' A few sulking pieces glinted in a worn hat that lay exhausted beside the writing. A priest stopped to talk to the young man, whose expression was gentle; the two men were deep in conversation. I stood on the pavement opposite for several minutes watching the scene. Passers-by stared at the young man first with curiosity then with disapproval. A small Frenchman in a grey coat and hat muttered to his wife as they passed, 'They are all the same these young people. They think the world owes them a living.' And so what if they do, I thought to myself and smiled. I felt more than sympathy for the young man; I liked him. I felt bound to him by youth. We were both young and we both had time, he to write provocative signs on the pavement, I to be arrogant and independent. I was with him all the way and I wanted to cross the street and tell him so. But I walked on. Yet the scene told me that at least I had come to a city where people were not afraid to show what they felt.

Before I left the bridge I turned to watch fat, white clouds move across the pale sky, carrying with them the pink light from the winter sun. The still, grey water of the Seine held the un-steady reflections of the bare trees and ornate buildings. The Cathedral of Notre-Dame rose from the Ile de la Cité, solitary and magnificent as it deigned to glitter in the feeble sunlight.

In my mind I moved from Hugo's novel, *The Hunchback of Notre-Dame*, and the sound of cathedral bells, through a Renoir

35

painting of the bustling streets of Paris to the reality of the
Beatles' record *A Hard Day's Night* that rang out from the
American drugstore on the Boulevard Saint Germain. The
pavement was crowded with attractive girls in wide brimmed felt
hats and bright clothes, with odd students and tall, cool young
men. Faces peered from the windows of the famous café opposite, Les Deux Magots, while the cheerful squat church of Saint
Germain seemed indifferent to the vibrating scene. The Paris I
had known at my Convent, where I had spent my fourteenth
year, had confined itself to Napoleon's tomb, the Eiffel Tower
and other such edifying monuments. At last I found myself in the
Paris I had longed to know, the Paris of Edith Piaf and Hemingway, the city of artists and thinkers, of passionate, articulate
individuals.

I stayed in the Rue Coetlogon near the heart of Saint Germain
where quiet alleys away from the main street led to gnarled
trees and squat eighteenth-century houses, to old street lamps
and cafés below street level. Two of my greatest friends, Irina
and Marina von Arnim, lived at Number Six. We had shared a
flat together in Rome; on no money we had lived an uproarious
life on semolina and black coffee. The two girls, twins, and
twenty-four years old, came from Berlin. Their family is famous
in German history, and before the war the von Arnims held great
estates in East Germany. My father had seen one of the estates
under strange circumstances. In 1945, having been a prisoner
for four years, he and several thousand other RAF officers began
their long march through East Germany as the Germans re-
treated before the Russian armies. For one night the long
columns of men stopped at Muskau, a beautiful country house
set in a great park. Muskau was the property of Irina's uncle,
who died a few years later, a Russian prisoner in Siberia. Three
months after my trip to Paris I was staying with his daughter in
Berlin.

Irina and Marina had left Berlin at eighteen and had earned
their living as interpreters in French, German, English and
Italian. I now found them learning Spanish and perusing Russian
grammar books. The twins did not resemble each other greatly
though they both had strong faces and frank eyes. In character
they were quite different; Irina was impulsive, strong willed and
interested in politics, while Marina was gentle and wise. Both

had enormous vitality and courage. I loved being with them again but we saw little of each other for they both worked exceedingly hard. I was left to discover Paris for myself.

I was late for my appointment with Alain, a French friend in his fourth year at the Institute of Political Science. The building was close to the café, Les Deux Magots, where we had arranged to meet. I found him alone at a table wearing the respectable suit that he always wore, reading *Le Monde* through heavy black rimmed glasses. I made my apologies and we ordered black coffee at four shillings a cup, not a price that Hemingway could have afforded. I envied him so much, a student in Paris. I asked him about his studies.

'You have to work six to eight hours a day, but it is fascinating. The lecturers are men famous in their professions as lawyers or political writers.' I knew the course in political science was exacting. The entrance examination is highly competitive and anyone who gets in is regarded as exceptionally clever, but I had not expected quite such seriousness. 'Don't you have any fun?' I asked. Alain looked at me with pity. 'Harriet, you are in France not England. I know that you do no work at university in England. I have a friend at Oxford and I have seen his exams. They are nothing compared with ours. In France you have to work to get ahead.'

Though the Institute of Political Science is incorporated in the University of Paris Alain took no part in university life. His comments were like a cold shower. Of the clubs, he said, ' ridiculous,' of the student theatre, ' nothing but amateur theatricals.' He went on, ' I don't know why they bother when Paris has the best theatre in the world.' Alain condemned student politics as ' childish '. He was a tremendous admirer and supporter of de Gaulle. On America he poured invective, on France undiluted praise; on England he showered his pity.

'Life in France is straightforward because it is a meritocracy,' he announced. 'Those who are bright get to the top. Those who are not must take second best.' The brightest students, he told me went to the *Grandes Écoles*, adult boarding schools of university standard, though quite separate from the University of France. The *Grandes Écoles* are Napoleonic institutions and Frenchmen sigh at the very sound of their name. Some teach economics and mathematics; the ENA (École Nationale d'Administration) trains the future civil servants of France. Most courses last only two years, but the entrance examinations are the hardest in France. The Institute of Political Science does not rival the *Grandes Écoles* in prestige. Nevertheless it also has a competitive entrance examination and reckons on some of the most intelligent French students.

'The *Grandes Écoles* and the Institute of Political Science take the cream of French students so there isn't much left for the University of Paris,' Alain explained. 'It has to be content with a surfeit of girls and of the less bright young men.' The Faculty of Law, however, was an exception. Law was not taught at any of the *Grandes Écoles* and so the Faculty had a monopoly of students. 'As you know,' he went on, 'there is no selective system for university. Anyone who has passed his *baccalauréat* can go. It could not be more fair. Students with the best qualifications get the best jobs.'

The next day I descended to lower spheres, to the heart of the University of Paris, the Sorbonne, where I could breathe easily.

In bright, cold sunshine I walked through the gates of the Jardin du Luxembourg. I kept to the stone path and watched the frost sparkle under the morning light. Solitary figures sat on park benches looking at the fountains, at the wide expanse of green grass, at the statues and alcoves, at the imposing Senate building. As I approached the Boulevard Saint Michel that lay on the other side of the park I was overtaken by a group of young people carrying books under their arms. They ran up the steps that led on to the street and I followed. As I emerged from the silent park on to the Boulevard Saint Michel, the centre of Sorbonne life, I felt transported into the heart of the student world. The pavements were alive with running feet; voices, cars, laughter echoed in the streets. In the cold morning air students stood in front of book shops, pawn shops, clothes shops announcing cheap buys, stamping their feet and blowing into their hands to keep warm. Off the street, behind the plate glass window of the corner café, faces protected from the cold wind followed the figures outside. Sweet stalls blocked the pavements and the sticky aroma of toffee apples merged with the irresistible smell of hot chestnuts from an old iron barrow parked in a side street.

My eye caught the sign, Rue de la Sorbonne, and crossing the road I turned into the narrow street and joined the steady flow of students filing along the pavement under the shadow of the high walls of the Sorbonne buildings. To my surprise, as we approached the entrance gates, I saw a Black Maria, and on the far pavement twenty policemen standing in groups outside the main doors. In the Place de la Sorbonne directly opposite, the pensive statue of Robert de la Sorbonne looked on in disapproval. Once inside the courtyard of the University building I understood the reason for the presence of the *gendarmes*. A meeting had been called to protest against the inadequacy of the University reforms put forward in the *Plan Fouchet*. Two hundred students crowded round the loudspeakers and banners that were installed on the steps joining the forecourt of the church to the main courtyard. The guardians of these steps, statues of French philosophers, were used as props for the amplifiers.

The meeting had been organised by the *Union Nationale des Étudiants Français*, the student representative body that provided the link between students and the administration. In an atmosphere of excitement and curiosity the speakers – some were teachers, others leaders of the UNEF – delivered their violent attacks, shaking their fists and shouting to daunt the fierce hecklers. I was delighted to find such a lively meeting. It seemed that Paris was still, as it always has been, the centre of political ferment. Fouchet was bitterly attacked. In France scholarships and grants are few and poorer students have to work to be able to study. Under the new plan several classes will become compulsory, and the UNEF claimed that poorer students would have to leave university because they could not attend lectures and hold on to their jobs. Hecklers shouted that special provisions for working students had been made but other voices answered that the provisions were inadequate. At the end of the meeting, a fiery, bearded boy, shouting and shaking his fist, called for united action against the Plan, and a roar of approval rose in the courtyard. But there was no disorder and gradually the crowd disbanded, filing through the gates into the confusion of the Boulevard Saint Michel.

Inquisitive, I wandered through the corridors of the Sorbonne, the original University of Paris. Today it houses most of the Faculty of Letters and the Faculty of Science. I called on a branch office of the UNEF in the Philosophy Department. An official of the union explained that French student politics were even more intricate than French national politics. 'You name it and we've got it,' he said laughing. Besides the normal Marxist, Trotskyist and Gaullist or Centre Party groups, the Sorbonne boasts an active group of Fascists, Isolationists, and a Revolutionary Committee. The UNEF tries to incorporate them all but, the official sighed, 'We feel much like General de Gaulle when he said that it was impossible to govern a country with two hundred and fifty different sorts of cheese.'

The professors found it equally difficult to keep track of student politics. 'The leaders are never the same from one week to another,' said Monsieur Vedel, *Doyen* of the Faculty of Law. 'One day I received the "Executive" in my office. A neat, smart girl appears with two well dressed young men. A week later the "Executive" had another appointment, only this time a girl with knee length hair and trousers caked with paint appeared at the door followed by two beatnik friends. "What has happened to your predecessors?" I asked, and one replied, "Last night there was a coup d'état and we took control of the organisation."'

'There is no unity among students – yet,' an official of UNEF told me. We were sitting in the Café de la Sorbonne overlooking the noisy square cluttered with motorcycles. 'Our organisation tries to co-ordinate student opinion so we can present proposals that have the support of the majority.' The *Plan Fouchet* was at the heart of the new crisis. In lucid and concise French he criticised the reform programme; it was unfair to students who had to support themselves; it increased the pressure of work; it reduced the little academic freedom that there was by limiting the choice of subjects. 'They are trying to push us into slots,' the young man said severely. Many people I spoke to felt that the Fouchet plan, though it attempted to tackle the problem of overcrowding, took no account of the dull curricula and the absence of communication. I was very surprised to find so much criticism and concrete thought on educational reform. At the Sorbonne I felt little of the agreeable apathy of Aix.

'People are generally waking up,' a Psychology student told me. I had seen advertisements for political meetings and discussions, also for the latest plays by the Sorbonne theatre groups, the

Théâtre Ancien and the Théâtre Moderne; film shows, painting exhibitions, works of sculpture, music recitals, I had heard and read of all these. Though only a minority of students took part in university life I was aware of a nucleus of active and critical students whose influence might be contagious. I hoped so.

There was even some life going on at the *Cité Universitaire*, the depressing student suburb composed of drab, hideous *pavillons* and *maisons*. Pierre, a tall gaunt figure with sunken eyes, was an actor in the theatre group at the *Cité*. ' *On recommence à penser*,' he meditated as we talked in the garden. 'We've listened to Papa de Gaulle long enough. Now we have some ideas of our own.'

I was glad to find myself once again in the chaos of the Boulevard Saint Germain, and decided to call on my greatest French friend, Hugues de Jouvenel, who lived in a charming flat overlooking a courtyard, two minutes from the Deux Magots. Hugues was in his second year of law; we had known each other since we were children, for his father, a Professor in Political Thought at the Faculty of Law and a famous writer, was a great friend of my father. Hugues, tall, thin, with dark eyes and a slightly cynical expression, agreed to take me to the new Faculty of Law, close to where both he and I lived, in the Rue d'Assas. Hugues spent most of his time at the new Faculty and seldom crossed the beautiful Jardin du Luxembourg to the old Faculty in the Place du Panthéon, where lectures are held for fourth year students, and where the *Doyen* holds court.

A gigantic modern building suddenly loomed above the low houses in the Rue d'Assas. Six policemen stood talking to each other at the entrance. I followed Hugues into the entrance hall. It might have been a race track at the end of the day. The floor was littered with pamphlets and paper, whipped up by the draught as it blew from the open doors. Wall after wall blazed with the invitations to every conccivable function. The architecture was impressive, particularly in the main amphitheatre built for over sixteen hundred students. As we sat waiting to hear one of the most famous law professors, Monsieur Duverger, I felt a cinerama film would be more appropriate than a lecture.

Monsieur Duverger spoke on the role of advertising in modern society. How long could French television resist a commercial channel? Did not advertising demand the use of every mass medium? Was not television subject, like any business concern, to the dictates of economics? Monsieur Duverger went on to discuss the role of advertising in communist countries. 'Six hundred thousand Chinese,' he began, but before he could finish his sentence a cry went up, ' *et moi, et moi, et moi*,' thus completing the title of the rage song by the French pop singer Antoine, *Six Hundred Million Chinese and Me and Me and Me.*

The students listened with interest to Monsieur Duverger. They applauded, or whistled if they did not agree, particularly at the end of the lecture when Monsieur Duverger, with humour, suggested that in capitalist countries the liberties of the individuals would be increasingly curtailed, whereas in communist countries they would increase, and thus the two societies would grow similar. Boos echoed from the corners of the hall and Monsieur Duverger, smiling and amused, rose from his seat and was escorted from the lecture hall by a man in uniform, dressed like the Black Rod of the House of Commons in knickerbockers with a shiny gold medal hanging from his neck. From what I could gather he was a university retainer whose duty it was to protect the professors; from what no one seemed sure. 'Law students may shout a great deal, above all in lectures, but they are not violent,' Hugues said with a touch of scorn. He saw the 'Black Rod' more as a human alarm clock, a sign to the professor that the lecture should end, than as a bodyguard.

The hall emptied and we followed the throng up five flights of stairs to the student restaurant. I was forewarned. 'You will now taste some of the worst food in France,' Hugues announced solemnly as we joined the queue. I dragged a tray with a hot, white plate along the brass ledge. An obliging lady threw a piece of tired meat on to it, as one might throw a flat stone in the water hoping to make it bounce on the surface before sinking. The next server took aim with a ladle full of mashed potato that exploded on top of the meat. A third, standing at least a foot away from my tray, scooped a ladle full of lentils out of a tin drum and took aim. But alas, she missed, and most of the lentils landed in slimy pools on the tray itself. I picked up my tray and was about to walk towards a table when the unsmiling server looked at my black fur beret and mumbled, 'No hats in here.' 'No hats, why?' 'Custom,' she said peremptorily.

Hugues began to laugh. ' I forgot; it's one of the old traditions of the restaurant. Any girl who walks in wearing a hat is greeted with a chant " *chapeau, chapeau* " from all the boys, who bang on the table with their forks, until she takes off her hat. The origin of the custom is unknown but it still survives.'

During lunch Hugues spoke of the competition at the Faculty. ' Pressure is enormous; only twenty per cent of students pass their examinations each year. My friends work tremendously hard and have really very little spare time. Perhaps this is why there is so little university life among law students.' I was struck by the atmosphere outside the dining hall : glum faces wandered along corridors, tired people climbed the stairs. The energy of the lecture hall had vanished. I passed a notice board to which clung giant health posters. ' Come to our health centre in the Alps.' ' Do not let work run you down. Find a balanced life in the peace of the Aix Valley.' ' Pay us a visit and face your examinations with courage.'

However, many teachers and professors felt that the image of the ' over-worked student ' was an unjustified concoction of post war France. I called on Mademoiselle Geslin, a charming woman with a dry sense of humour, who had taught French at my Convent. More than any teacher I have ever known, she inspired me with a deep love of literature. She was baffled by the attitude of her own students.

' Why is it that the young French are so afraid of exams?' she said with despair. ' We had the same amount of work and the same examinations, whatever they say, but we were much braver. To fail an exam was not the end of the world; today it calls for a mental collapse.' I remembered the fear I had seen at the Convent as examinations approached; I also remembered the mass cheating. My friends had mathematical theorems hidden in their stockings, written on their knees and on the palms of their hands. In the higher classes too, the same indiscriminate cheating was a well known fact.

' All my classes cheat, or try to,' Mademoiselle Geslin admitted. ' I think the French have grown very devious since the war. Children admire the underhand methods of the Resistance, and in the same vein they take up cheating at school.' Mademoiselle accepted cheating but she was persistently disappointed at the spinelessness in her students. ' In *troisième* I teach neurotic girls of only fourteen, who at the very mention of the word *bacca-laureát* start to shake at the knees. *Il leur faut un peu de courage.*' (They need a bit of courage.)

Monsieur Vedel also thought that French students exaggerated the mental strain. At his office in the Panthéon he told me, 'This whole question of competition is a lot of rubbish. There is no more competition in French universities than there is in any other European university.' Monsieur Vedel estimated that over a third of the students enrolled in his Faculty did not even present themselves at the examinations. Of the remaining two thirds, over half passed their examinations either in June or in October. 'I was asked to make a report for a member of parliament, giving statistical information as to the number of failures each year. The net result of the inquiry was that of serious students, that is students who want to pass examinations, three out of five are successful.'

Monsieur Vedel had also been asked to comment on a possible *numerus clausus*. 'We have never had a *numerus clausus*. Where we differ from English universities is that we do not impose any entrance requirements, therefore selection falls at examination times.' Like Professor Wolfe at Toulouse, Monsieur Vedel felt that with the implementation of the *Plan Fouchet* the situation in French universities would radically change. Non-serious students would not be allowed to stay on. Monsieur Vedel told me that many undergraduates enrolled at the university only to help their parents who then paid less taxes and could claim national assistance.

'But these children have no intention of doing any work. Most of them take a job and appear once a week for their *Travaux Pratiques*, an obligatory class for all students.' Stricter selection would mean more space and would give greater chance for individual attention. Monsieur Vedel hoped for a corresponding increase in degrees. 'France needs more graduates. I cannot fill the demand from industrial firms.' He added with emphasis, 'The truth is that France is not as dependent on examinations as people think. Good jobs which demand fewer qualifications are not so hard to come by.'

I did not find a single student who agreed with him. Catherine Courroux, a very clever girl who had been a great friend of mine at the Convent, felt that examinations were all-important. 'You cannot get any sort of interesting job without a degree, and even then, without a post-graduate degree you will be lucky to find a good job. For business, banking, industry, you must have academic qualifications.' Catherine explained that competition would not be so acute if there were other outlets for talent, 'But opportunity in France is limited. I study French at the university and I must become a teacher. There is no other profession open to me.'

A friend of Catherine's, a student of sociology, had another explanation. 'In France, where seventeen per cent of the population lives on the land and industry is under-developed, there is no demand for the small private businesses that need inventiveness and originality more than a university degree. The English are lucky in the boutiques, the eccentric shops and the art galleries that absorb the unacademic young.'

Dominique, a very pretty French girl whom I had met in England, the daughter of a publisher and a first-year history student at the Sorbonne, felt that the specialisation had got out of hand. 'You can hardly become a secretary without a degree,' she told me sadly. 'And even for newspaper work you must have a diploma from a school of journalism.'

Advertising firms take a more elastic attitude to examinations. I met one young man who had failed his *baccalauréat,* gone into an advertising firm in Paris and now, three years later, held a good job. ' In my work a university education is no asset. You aren't likely to dream up a catchy phrase to promote dog food in a Sorbonne lecture on Racine.'

The spearhead of this era is the new Faculty of Nanterre that will one day be the university for northern Paris. Catherine was enrolled there, not out of choice, but under the new law she was allowed to apply only to the university closest to her home. We took a bus at the Pont de Neuilly, and half an hour later alighted on a marsh. Deep mud surrounded the tall modern buildings that rose above the bleak waste land on the outskirts of Paris. Perhaps to compensate for the depressing surroundings, Nanterre had the latest equipment: closed circuit television linking lecture halls, a well designed theatre, and most curious of all, 'live' blackboards. The professor wrote on a small pad in front of him and his writing was projected onto a screen behind him, thus making chalk and a blackboard obsolete.

A professor who taught both at Nanterre and Paris told me that whereas only fifty students visited him in a year in Paris, over five hundred came to see him at Nanterre. 'At Nanterre,' he said 'each professor has his own room where he can receive his students.' Catherine felt that at Nanterre students might at last establish some personal contact with their professors.

Nanterre wore the 'new look', not only in education. The Nanterre theatre, only two years old, is one of the most enterprising student theatres in France. I spoke to the Director who planned to take the company on a tour of Germany in the summer. His repertoire included Beckett, Pinter, Wesker and Brecht. 'We are in close contact with the Sorbonne theatres, the Théâtre Ancien and the Théâtre Moderne, but we think we are more avant garde.'

The advertisements that filled the bill-boards were undoubtedly more dashing than those at the Sorbonne. 'Psychology and sex' 'Sex and religion' 'Are morals effete?' – all screamed for attention. Psychology, sociology, urbanology discussions were advertised, as well as talks on the experimental theatre and experimental art.

Even this pacemaker faculty has not escaped the pressure of competition. As examinations approached, on a foggy day when the faculty buildings looked more like water towers in a bog, a boy in his first year had thrown himself out of a window. 'We shall all go mad unless they slow the pace,' Catherine said with feeling. Her course comprised eight obligatory lessons a week and sixteen supplementary lectures.

It was strange that Marc Antoine Squarciafici should be so critical of the educational system; with outstanding academic qualifications he would undoubtedly benefit under its rules. But Marc Antoine was one of the many non-conformists who transformed my image of Paris, who repainted its portrait in unpredictable, provocative colours, who rumbled beneath the surface of the city questioning and criticising the standard views.

I had been given Marc Antoine's address by a great friend, who often spoke of his academic brilliance. He had finished a degree in Law and another in Political Science and was about to take his *Agrégation* in Economics, as a prelude to his doctorate, which he hoped to prepare in the following year. He spoke fluent Russian and Chinese and was preparing examinations in both languages concurrently at two different language schools. I was not surprised when he said, 'I don't have much free time.' I called on Marc Antoine at his mother's flat in the Quai d'Orsay. He appeared wearing a dark green velvet coat. 'I have a slight cold,' he apologised, ' but it is nothing serious.' Three days later he was in bed with jaundice.

Marc Antoine had spent a year at the Beaux Arts studying architecture before he went to the Institute of Political Science. He had detested the *Bisutage,* an active 'let's be beastly to the freshmen' campaign on the part of the older students. The *Bisutage* lasted much of the year and prevented all first year students from working. Marc Antoine had learned so little at the end of his first year that he left. All in all his undergraduate life had been disappointing. ' Either you must lead a solitary existence or possibly an intimate existence but never a gregarious existence. French students dislike crowds.'

Now that he was no longer an undergraduate he was still depressed by Paris and Parisians. 'This is quite simply not a city of opportunity,' he announced, ' you feel this country is expanding neither creatively nor industrially. Enterprise seems to stagnate.' Even though he spoke fluent Chinese and Russian and had high academic qualifications, Marc Antoine said it would be difficult for him to find an interesting job. 'Many French people speak Russian and though I've looked, I can't find anyone who has the slightest use for Chinese. I've tried several businesses and the Foreign Office but it seems that Chinese is obsolete.'

He was also depressed by Paris snobbery. 'This city is appallingly snobbish. Many of my friends spend their lives in the same tiny circle. It is a poor reflection on our great meritocracy, that people of talent should still be ostracised by Paris " society " because of their background.' At the university Marc Antoine had found the same exclusiveness. ' The upper class students didn't mix with the others but kept to their small cliques.'

' I long to leave Paris,' Marc Antoine exclaimed. He planned to go to America as soon as he had finished his doctorate. ' I've applied to Harvard Business School and I'm waiting for an answer.' Life in the venerated capital of France did not suit

Hugues either. ' *On n'est pas libre à Paris,*' he said deliberately.
' In London [where he studied for a year] I went with friends
to Westminster Bridge in the early hours of the morning.
We played cards on the pavement and watched the first
light of dawn paint the water with its orange glow. We read
Wordsworth's " Sonnet to the New Day ". Not one passer-
by gave us so much as a look. But in Paris, *cela ne se fait pas.*'

Hugues wrote incessantly. His first book of poetry was being
published later that year. On his shelves lay an agglomeration
of novels, philosophic works of all eras, modern French, English
and German poetry. Soon after I arrived he organised a dinner
party so that I could meet his university friends. The evening
passed imperceptibly as we discussed painting, writing and philosophy, though not in any philosophic frame of mind for our
heated arguments had twice caused the neighbours to complain.
At five in the morning I was sitting on the floor of the flat,
propped up against the back of a chair, listening to a passionate
argument on the comparative merits of Proust and Virginia
Woolf. Empty glasses lined the bookcases; thick cigarette smoke
curled around the naked light bulbs. Plates were stacked in a
corner and a half empty bowl of tired salad stood by the door.
To end the long evening we all decided to walk through the
quiet streets of Paris. Outside, the dark sky was streaked with
the first light from the winter sun; rain fell slowly on the grey
pavements, and in the air was the hint of freshly made croissants.
I had never been so happy in Paris before. I had found my own
movable feast.

One day Hugues announced, ' I shall show you my Paris.'
That evening Hugues, myself and Gérard, Hugues's greatest
friend, went in search of a place to eat. The old lamps of Saint
Germain lit the narrow streets overcast with strange shadows
from irregular roofs. We passed enigmatic restaurants and cafés,
La Petite Chaise, Le Temps Perdu, hidden in alleyways like
raisins in a pudding. Finally we went into the Crêperie, with a
façade that came from a page of *The Three Musketeers*, and
feasted on pancakes.

'And now to our haunt,' Hugues announced and we piled
into his car and drove to the Club des Poètes in the Seventh
Arrondissement. As we arrived I was given a card that read, *On*

y rencontre les poètes d'aujourd'hui et ceux de demain. (Here you meet the poets of today and the poets of tomorrow). We passed under a low door and came into a room lit by red lights. A spotlight focused on the face of a girl who spoke in a low voice. She had reached the climax of her sad poem and looked as if she were about to cry.

We took our places at one of the tables. The Club might have been any café; the room was small and about thirty people sat at benches and tables. The Director of the Club came up to talk to Hugues and Gérard whom he obviously knew well. He was in his late thirties, a lively and amusing man. I learned that once a month he had his own television programme in which he presented any poet he thought interesting. He had asked Gérard to appear in the following month, a great compliment since few of his poets were students.

We listened to several poems recited by their authors. I liked some very much; they were unsentimental, at times witty, and perceptive in the Maupassant tradition, neither negative nor despairing like so much modern poetry. At one point Gérard stood in the throw of the spotlight and recited a strange, realistic poem on the countryside in unusual staccato verse. Both Gérard and Hugues felt that the Club des Poètes offered artistic freedom that was no longer innate in the city of Paris. Gérard felt that the authoritarian hand of de Gaulle was strangling the arts. 'In the meritocracy of de Gaulle there is little room for the arts,' he said sadly.

Nonconformists seemed unanimous in their dislike of de Gaulle. To Hugues and his friends de Gaulle threatened the arts, to Marc Antoine he stifled opportunity, and to many young Europeans, some of the most interesting and intelligent people I have ever met, he was the great obstacle to European unity. In a small café near the Panthéon I met Gérard Fuchs, the head of the young European Federalist movement in Paris. He was not satisfied with a mere economic union, but still held to the more traditional concept of a political federation of all the countries of Western Europe.

'To me a federal Europe is the most thrilling conception of our age; it could be the start of a new civilisation that is neither based on communism as it is in the East, nor on the extreme form of capitalism as it is in the West. Europe could provide the inspiration for a renaissance in ideas and culture. Despite what de Gaulle tells us, the future of France lies in a European federation, for we belong neither to the West nor to the East and still less can we afford to pursue a policy of isolation.'

I met several other staunch Europeans through Professor Bertrand de Jouvenel, Hugues's father. He is one of the most well-known and articulate practical thinkers in Europe; that day, and on most days, he wore his gardening clothes, baggy trousers and an old sweater. He looked absent-minded and immensely distinguished with his pointed white beard, straight nose, heavy white eyebrows and unrestrained smile.

After a brilliant lecture on the early influence of Marx, delivered contrary to French tradition as an opinion and not as a stream of information to be learned by heart, delighted students came up to congratulate him. I had never seen this happen before. It struck me that if there were more teachers like him, the whole face of French universities might change. Students need only a little encouragement to respond. I missed the professor, who suddenly left the building. I stood perplexed but when I told Hugues he laughed. ' It was Saturday,' he said simply. ' And on Saturday afternoon my father rushes from the Faculty to a friend's house where he can watch his beloved football on television.'

I attended another lecture a week later. Professor de Jouvenel, to the surprise of everyone, appeared at the entrance of the auditorium in a black suit, his black shoes shining, and the top of a white handkerchief showing from his breast pocket. '*Aujourd'hui il a un rendez-vous*,' I heard a student whisper. People around me seemed amused by his eccentricities. The professor was deep in conversation with three young men. He called me over to him. ' Harriet, I want you to meet these fascinating young men, and I suggest that you all go and drink a cup of coffee together. They can tell you all you want to know about the university.' The young men who had come from far to hear Jouvenel looked amazed. '*Mais Monsieur, le cours*.' ' My lecture is of no importance,' the professor said decidedly. ' A coffee will do you more good,' and with that he left us in the corridor and walked into the lecture hall, closing the door behind him.

Professor de Jouvenel could not have chosen three more interesting individuals. Gérard, the most humorous, was a leading member of the Federalist movement, and was preparing a degree in European Studies. The University Centre for European Studies, to which universities all over Europe are affiliated, is situated in Paris. The courses deal with the legal and administrative aspects of the Common Market, with European history and government. Patrice and Daniel were carrying out a survey among members of parliament to gauge interest in a federation of Europe.

The three did not entirely agree. Patrice and Gérard hoped for a politically united Europe governed by a European parliament, that would stabilise the balance of power between East and West. Daniel thought Europe should remain as it was, an economic Common Market, not a political federation. They all wanted England to join the Common Market, though Patrice admitted that politically he thought Europe would be better off without her.

All three felt a tremendous sense of urgency to create a united Europe. 'Europe must unite now. There is no time to lose. If England could join soon we would welcome her, but Europe can't wait for her,' said Daniel with conviction. Patrice spoke strongly against the policy of de Gaulle which seemed designed to keep England out, 'But,' he went on ' this would never have happened if England had signed the Treaty of Rome.'

French and foreign students alike paid little heed to the views of the General. Sue Collins had recommended Art Eggendorf as the typical American in Paris, but I should have known that Sue had very strange ideas. Art, twenty-three, with blond hair and blue eyes, told me, 'De Gaulle can go to hell; he won't get me out of Paris.' He came from Harvard where he had taken a law degree Magnum Cum Laude. He shared a flat with a French undergraduate in the troisième arrondissement, loved Paris, and got on wonderfully with the French.

I rang Art on Sue's instruction and asked if I could talk to him. I could hear Robert, his flat mate, whisper, 'But who is she? How old is she? Is she pretty?' Art covered the mouthpiece with his hand and said, 'Don't be crazy, I can't ask her that over the telephone.'

The troisième arrondissement is not a student quarter. It is an area of small shop keepers, of chemists' shops, butchers and bakeries and market stalls that clutter the small, dirty streets. I had hardly stepped into the flat, glanced at the big studio with unframed canvases suspended on the walls, when Art led me down the stairs into the street to do the shopping. In an alley that might have been part of Soho, Art walked swinging his shopping bag, talking to passers by. An alsatian stood at the corner of the street. As we approached the dog Art asked me when I was leaving Paris. 'March 15th,' I said. 'The Ides of March,' he muttered. Then he stopped and stared at the dog. 'Beware of the Ides of March, do you hear,' he said in a loud voice, and the enormous alsatian yelped in fear and ran off down the street.

Art waved to pedestrians, and laughed and talked to the shop-keepers who knew him well, and shook their heads despairingly. 'Not a cross face in the whole street,' he said as we walked to-wards the flat. 'If I behaved like a lunatic in England, people would call a policeman, in the States I would get a knife in my back. But here no one cares.' He added sarcastically, 'The frogs could hardly think worse of us anyway.'

The only person not to appreciate Art was his landlady. She called in the police every time he and Daniel gave a party. 'She screams if you sneeze on the stairs. She can't stand noise. One day she got mad at me for not saying *bonjour*. Now I say it to her all the time, particularly in the evening. In the blackness of the night I clasp her hand and say *bonjour, bonjour, bonjour*.'

We got back to the flat and Art overcooked the meat. As I pulled the black, steaming joint out of the oven he looked at me with a threatening expression and said that at least it wouldn't matter to me, because in England they always overcooked the meat.

The sky was grey on my last day in Paris. Hugues decided to give a small farewell dinner party. We concocted the menu together. That day Hugues insisted on speaking English, as he was wont to do in his more optimistic moods. I was to buy the cheese, the fruit, the lettuce and the tomatoes for a salad, he agreed to buy the wine, the bread and the eggs for an exotic omelette. At seven o'clock I arrived at his flat with a large paper package. I put it on his table and started to pull out my mer-chandise. His face fell and, as I put the last tomato on the table, he put his hand to his head in dismay. '*Mon Dieu*, I thought I was to buy all that,' and pointed to his package that bulged with exactly the same food. We both burst out laughing, and the *entente cordiale* survived a slightly monotonous meal, soon forgotten if not digested, in a long evening of hysterical jokes, passionate discussions, and bottle after bottle of *vin ordinaire*.

3

Rome

February 1967

In the new year I went to Italy. I was escorted from Ventimiglia
on the Italian border by a thick fog and, for a memorable mile,
by two enormous policemen on motor cycles who screeched in
front of my Mini, forcing me to stop, and demanded four thousand lire for exceeding the speed limit. I spent the night in
Florence and arrived in Rome in time for lunch on a Sunday
morning in January.

I was so delighted to be back in Rome again that I almost
wanted to shake hands with pedestrians and say to them *Sono
tornata.*

The familiar streets, churches and the intoxicating atmosphere that came from nowhere stoked my memory; reminiscences flooded my thoughts. At sixteen I had spent six glorious
months living in the old part of the city at Number One, Piazza
San Salvatore in Lauro. The square was made up of low, russet
red houses that stood in the shadow of a majestic church built
in grey stone with wide steps and high columns. Fresh flowers
from a flower stall filled the air with sweetness, black haired
Italian children played on the steps of the church. The Piazza
led on to a famous street of antique shops, the Via dei Coronari,
narrow, cobbled, with old fashioned lamps, sheltered from
sun and rain by overhanging roofs. I lived with two sisters, Litta
and Germana and their beautiful alsatian dog, though when I
addressed him in my abominable Italian he howled and left
the room.

Apart from learning Italian I wanted to study as much art
as possible. Twice a week I went to the Via Margutta, the famous artists' street, to Madame Hélène Zelezni-Scholz, an Hun-

54

garian sculptress of over eighty who gave lessons in clay modelling. Madame Zelezni had a beautiful face, thin, pale, with high cheek bones and gentle, laughing, brown eyes.

'I shall teach your eyes to see,' she told me the first day I arrived. At the time I did not know what she meant but I was soon to learn. I stared and stared at pictures and statues but did not notice the subtle shadows and muscles, until she pointed them out. She trained my eyes to connect different parts of the anatomy, to understand conjunction of shadow. In her studio that was filled with her own works, studies of hands, Madonnas in bronze, heads, bas-reliefs, I spent many desperate hours. I evolved deep sympathy for the artist in Virginia Woolf's book, *To The Lighthouse*, who grows so despondent as she watches her paint brush decimate the perfect image she holds in her mind. I struggled to copy Greek heads from art books. One effort resembled at its best a Zulu warrior and in a fit of rage I pulled the soft clay apart and reduced it to a ball of dough. Madame Zelezni was delighted. 'Excellent,' she cried. 'You should always destroy what you know is bad.' I muttered that I would have little to show at the end of the year if that were the case. In the coffee break at eleven I studied her works. Many had been commissioned for churches and public buildings. Later that year she did a bust of the Pope, who came for sittings in her small over-crowded studio.

Madame Zelezni was very direct. 'You look terrible this morning,' she would sometimes say to me. 'Your eyes are so little, very, very little. You have not slept enough,' she continued in her strong accent, 'and your skirt is too short. The knee joint always has been and always will be unaesthetic.'

I wanted to complement clay modelling with a more concrete knowledge of anatomy and chiaroscuro. To my delight I was admitted to the Free School of Art, the *Scuola Libera,* a branch of the Academy of Art open at no cost to anyone who passes the entrance examination. The School stood between the Via Ripetta, lined with Baroque churches and palaces, and the Tiber, bound by romantic bridges and traced with cargo boats. Throughout the spring I walked from the flat along the Tiber to my art school. The biting green of the riverside trees lit the surface of the grey water. The spring in Rome is sharp and strong.

In the large hall, Maria, the female model, sat in front of an electric fire surrounded by easels and stools. Foreign students stood in front of canvases splashing oils, middle-aged women bowed over their white sheets of paper drawing assiduously with coloured crayons. Artists, too poor to hire their own models, experimented patiently with new techniques and sighed for better days. Giovanni, a young painter in his thirties, had a black beard and cold grey eyes. 'The soul is in the hand,' he maintained solemnly as he painted enormous hands on black canvases. ' It is in the boots, van Gogh has proved it,' Signor Roberto insisted, an elderly gentleman who had painted all his life.

I learnt not from the Assistant Professor, who spent the morning doing crosswords, but from painters and students alike who were always ready to give advice. Bud, an American student, used to say, 'Be brave with your stick of charcoal. Get movement on to your page before detail.' I acquired a deep love of drawing in the hours that I spent in the friendly, relaxed atmosphere of the art school. However, Bud maintained that we needed variety and in the late spring I rode with him on the back of his motor bike to the parks where we set up our canvases in front of male statues.

But I did other things besides drawing. Through Litta I met a group of young Romans who lived in a roundabout of gaiety. I made wonderful friends and spent six months in a carefree world of hectic and hilarious fun. There were parties; dinners in Trastevere where I felt the presence of the Renaissance; crazy jaunts through the streets of Rome looking for a gay night club; there were visits to late night museums and tours of the city on warm spring evenings. At Easter I joined Sunday skiing expeditions. The coach left at six and I rarely got to bed on a Saturday night before three. Invariably I sat half asleep on the doorstep clutching my skis, dimly aware of the orange light of dawn.

The pace of life quickened with the warm weather. Pierre Andrea Magistrati, one of my greatest friends felt that heat precluded work. 'To the sea,' he cried, and we flew to Fregene or Ostia just outside Rome, where we spent lazy days on the beach eating ice cream and roasting in the sun. Released from Lenten abstention Italian girls gave dances and parties. In the evening we hurried back to Rome from the warm beach in time to change and dance through the night on a roof garden under the stars. Fabio, a tall, black-haired Neapolitan friend, decided one evening to drive to Naples. At six in the morning I found myself eating a delicious crisp pizza in a *trattoria* overlooking the Bay of Naples. The sun was low on the horizon; the water glimmered, Fabio murmured, 'Only in Naples can you get a good pizza.'

We ate pizzas at the party I gave. Each friend brought either wine, cakes or cheese. I made pancakes, called by my friends English pasta. Most were thrown out of the window and eaten by a hungry stray dog. At eight in the morning I had to clear the flat that seemed hit by a hurricane. In a daze, clutching my head for it tingled with the sounds of night, I threw paper plates at random down the garbage hatch, and, unknown to me, with them I tossed most of Litta's silver knives and forks. They were retrieved but I wasn't encouraged to give another party.

The whirlwind of gaiety was part of an attitude to life. My friends felt it a personal duty to enjoy themselves while they were young. 'The thoughts of youthful exploits will regale us in old age,' Pierre Andrea maintained. 'Most of us haven't hit on the catastrophes of life so we had better have fun while we can. If we don't laugh now we never will.' Time was short. 'Look at the women of Italy,' Fabio cried. 'At eighteen girls are *bellissima*, at thirty they are hideous.'

While I lived in Rome I breathed an atmosphere of laughter; now on a return visit a year and a half later I saw quite a different side of young Italian life. I spent most of my time at the university.

'Isn't it depressing!' Pierre Andrea said as we approached the entrance. It was built by Mussolini and stands as a monument to fascist architecture. I gazed through the entrance gate of square arches in heavy grey stone along a narrow avenue of trees and flower beds, obscured from the weak sun by piles of dead leaves and weeds that gardeners had forgotten. At the end of the avenue, in inimitable fascist pomposity, a massive grey block spread across the campus. To right and left russet brick buildings with iron window frames looked more like fall-out shelters than a university. Behind the main building, distinguished by a long flight of white stone stairs surmounted by a square jawed statue of Minerva, stretched an open expanse of ground the size of a football pitch. Dying tufts of grass sprouted from the brown earth and tired trees drooped in the morning sun.

Pierre Andrea knew the way to his own faculty but was unable to tell me anything about the other sombre buildings. ' I come here about twice a year to take examinations,' he announced. The majority of students ignore the clause in the statute book that requires obligatory attendance at all lectures. This utopian suggestion is not and could not be observed. Rome university was built for ten thousand students and today over sixty thousand are enrolled. There are no reading rooms, a bad library, no common rooms or study rooms. The student canteen holds only three hundred people and the biggest amphitheatre contains only five hundred seats so that anyone who fails to arrive early finds himself squatting in a gangway or balancing on a window sill at the back of the hall. First year students make an effort to attend lectures but are soon discouraged by the confusion and lack of space; in their second year they stay at home and study by themselves.

To take a degree a student must be enrolled at the university for four years and pass between seventeen and twenty-five examinations, according to his faculty. In either February or June he can offer himself for examination in as many subjects as he likes and can re-take an examination as often as he chooses. There is neither the room nor the staff for written examinations so all examinations are oral. They are mostly based on six-month lecture courses repeated twice a year. The courses are in turn based on books prescribed by, and often written by, the professors. I attended several lectures. First I tried Roman History. In the largest of the amphitheatres I struggled to the back of the hall, past the line of students standing in gangways, sitting on the floor by the windows. Try as I could I was neither able to see the Professor nor hear what he said, so I spent an unprofitable hour straining my ears and neck.

Next day I chose a lecture which I thought might be less well attended. It was on native habits in South America during the Middle Ages. I took a seat in a small uncrowded lecture hall. The professor did not appear, and thinking I might have mistaken the time of the lecture I consulted the girl beside me. ' Don't worry,' she said, ' the lecture should have begun twenty minutes ago but the Professor is always late. Sometimes he doesn't turn up at all.' However, a few minutes later, a good looking man of forty-five with greying hair and a moustache strode into the classroom and smiled benignly at the rows of students who rose in respectful silence. He took his seat and lit a Turkish cigarette which he placed in his long cigarette holder. As soon as he finished one cigarette he lit another and sat permanently shrouded in a thin veil of smoke. He spoke very slowly, grinning between puffs as he told amusing myths about native life in Brazil in the twelfth century. The more his class laughed the more pleased he seemed.

Whereas most students can choose which lectures they go to, those who read science and mathematics have no option. Their plight is desperate. One physics student described his laboratory where he carried out his practical work. ' There is no heating and the roof leaks, and what is more our equipment is antediluvian.'

All students suffer from the high cost of books. A History of Art student told me that she spent on an average seventy thousand lire (almost fifty-five pounds) on books alone each year. Then she paid out forty thousand lire in university taxes, and sixteen thousand lire on examination fees. The total was well over one hundred thousand lire (about seventy pounds), a huge amount for students who are not subsidised; only a fraction of Italian students are given grants or scholarships and this is one of their main bones of contention. To obtain a scholarship or grant a student has to keep up an average of twenty-five out of thirty marks in his work. If he falls below this average the grant is withdrawn and the poorer student has to leave the university and work. His richer contemporaries may be stupid but they can afford to stay on.

If the professors bestirred themselves and promoted a national campaign they might bring some order into the university life and make it more bearable for undergraduates; but the professors did not seem interested. Assistant professors and lecturers suffer as much as students from lack of space. They share offices and desks, have nowhere to see their pupils, or even store their books. A full professor, however, has an office to himself and an assistant. Gilberto, the head of the Student Parliament, told me that the professors are wary of joining any movement of reform because it might threaten their position. Many use their office and assistant for private research or business and are constantly on the defensive against any change that might upset their comfortable lives.

Some professors are active politicians. As I approached the entrance to the Faculty of Political Science with Pierre Andrea, I saw his face break into an enlightened smile. A black car stood near the main doors, a bored chauffeur leant on the bonnet glancing through a book.

'Today,' Pierre Andrea announced, 'we are honoured with the presence of Signor Moro, the President of the Consiglio, who among various occupations, including that of Prime Minister, also pursues that of a lecturer in Political Science. He should lecture twice a week but seldom comes twice a month. In his absence he sends his assistant.'

Besides the Prime Minister, the Foreign Minister and several members of the Senate held professorships. Gilberto said flatly, 'The title Professor brings extra money and prestige and a convenient place to work. They could not be less interested in the University.' 'They can't teach and they can't run the country,' snapped Pierre Andrea.

Later that day he took me to a faculty where examinations were in progress. Students filled the bare wooden corridors; the air was thick with cigarette smoke and laughter. At the far end of the passage a group clustered near a half open door. A friend of Pierre Andrea's, a young man with a stormy expression, came to meet us. 'I waited all day yesterday and was not called, and now I have been standing here since half past eight and it does not look as if I shall be called today either,' he said. I could not understand why the arrangements for examinations were so vague. Pierre Andrea explained.

Candidates who wished to take the examination submitted their names several months in advance. Later a list appeared announcing which candidates would be interviewed on which days. A precise time was not fixed and professors followed the rule: first come first served. 'The professor did not arrive until ten o'clock and he should have come at nine,' Pierre Andrea's friend continued. However, not all the students were so agitated.

One boy told me, ' As soon as all this is over I am going to Cortina to take a good look at this year's snow bunnies.' Nevertheless I heard bitter criticism of the system.

' It is a lucky dip,' said Fabio, a friend who studied Law. ' The professor opens one of the set books at any page and asks you a question relating to the paragraph in front of him. If you don't know the answer, though you might know everything else in the book, he can and often does fail you.' Emanuela, a Classics student and an old friend, felt that it was the mood that counted. ' If you are among the first to be examined or if you are called after lunch when the professor is feeling sleepy and sated, he might ask you some vague question about what aspect of your studies you found most interesting, and give you a pass mark whatever you say. If, however, you are called at the end of an arduous morning when he is tired and irritated, you are at his mercy.'

Most professors would have liked to hold written as well as oral examinations. ' But where would the students sit?' asked one simply. As it was, professors were inundated with six times the number of intended candidates and they found it increasingly difficult to give each one an adequate hearing. A normal oral examination should last at least twenty minutes. One female assistant in the History Department told me that she had worked with a professor who used to examine over sixty candidates in an afternoon, an average of six minutes for each.

The shortage of professors leads to the violation of University laws. The Statute Book decrees that at every session there must be three members of the Academic body, one of whom must be a professor. The others may be assistants or lecturers. This condition is frequently ignored. I spoke to many students who had not been examined by professors at all but by an assistant. Either the professor was away or too tired to go on. Pierre Andrea had sat twenty-six examinations but only three had been conducted according to the rules. At one examination he found only one assistant; the professor and his colleagues had gone out to lunch. Francesco, another friend, had found himself in the same position but refused to take the examination until the professor arrived.

By law all examinations are open to the public, but it was only after badgering a young assistant that I managed to get permission to attend one. Soon after nine in the morning I was shown into the examination room. The Head of the Department of Constitutional Law sat at a long table between two assistants. He offered a place in front of him and I sat down. He had a sharp, delicate face, polite manners and febrile hands that enacted his words as he spoke. His assistants were smart and loquacious, and reminded me of some of the elegant young men in Oscar Wilde's plays.

A few moments after I arrived a candidate entered the room and sat uneasily at the table. 'Good morning,' the Professor smiled, and then suddenly called for his coffee. The door opened and a porter came in. 'No more coffee sir, how about tea?' '*Dio mio*!' the Professor said, gesticulating. 'How can I start the day without my coffee? All right tea.' He turned to his Assistant. 'Rome is so agreeable in the winter don't you think?' The Assistant nodded and smiled. 'Did you read the article in the *Figaro* this morning?' he asked. The Professor nodded and gave an opinion. The student, a boy of twenty, with spectacles, a brown suit and red socks, sat pulling and stretching his fingers and intermittently biting his lips.

Eventually the Professor turned to his examinee and gave a sigh. '*Allora.*' He glanced at the three books on his desk. He had written one of them and it was his own book that he picked up and opened. 'What can you tell me about Locke and Hume and the influence of British philosophers on political theory?' The candidate looked aghast. He began to mumble and mutter and then lapsed into an exhausted silence.

'Well, didn't you study this chapter?' 'I didn't think that the English philosophers were important,' he said feebly. 'I learned about the French and Italians, just not the English.' The Professor looked quite unperturbed. His tea arrived. 'Thank you so much,' he said to the porter. With his teacup in his hand he addressed the young man. 'I don't really see how I can help you. The English philosophers, Locke and Hume, are fundamental. But you,' he added gravely, 'didn't think they were important.' For the next few minutes he discussed the extent of Locke's influence with one of the assistants, while the student pulled and stretched his fingers even harder.

'Is there really nothing you can tell me about Locke and Hume?' he repeated. The candidate looked desperate. Slowly the Professor put his cup down on the table. 'You had better come back when you have learned the significance of the English School,' and with a shrug of his shoulders he added, '*Mi dispiace, ma che posso fare?*' (I'm sorry but what can I do?) The disconsolate student left the room and in his examination book the Professor put a stroke, the irrevocable mark of failure. The next candidate was called for. The Professor leaned towards me and beaming said, ' I hope our other students will do better justice to English philosophers.'

The next examinee was better prepared. He knew what the book had to say about Locke. The Professor interrupted him and with a wry smile asked whether the student thought that Locke had an influence on the Constitutions of today. The boy looked worried and his appealing eyes seemed to say, 'That's not a fair question, that's not in the book.' The Assistant Professor ventured an answer. The Professor turned and began a discussion with the young man. They laughed and played with ideas as if they were sitting at a café in the sun, sipping lemon squash. The desperate examinee sat very still, waiting to be remembered. Finally the Professor turned to him and said in a cheerful voice, ' I hope you were listening to our discussion. You would have learned something,' and then continued the examination. Nervously the student answered the questions put to him, trying to gauge from the face of the examiner whether he was doing well or not. After ten minutes he was asked to leave the room.

'Well, what do you think?' said the examiner to his Assistant. Oral examinations are marked out of thirty and the pass mark is eighteen. 'He knew most of it. Twenty-two.' 'Perhaps twenty-four.' 'No, he was too hesitant.' 'Well, let's say twenty-three, and then we shall both be happy.'

I asked several professors if they thought that the examination system was a fair judge of intelligence. ' It is the best we can do in the circumstances,' one said. Another shook his head and answered, ' The situation has got out of hand. It is difficult to know what to do.'

Gilberto knew how to solve the problem. He was a small black-haired Italian, with fine features and quick eyes, and one of the most intelligent students I met. ' The professors are paralysed by their conservatism. It applies to most of the older generation. Many parents are slow to accept the idea of change, partly because they grew up in a Fascist society, in a climate of intolerance, and have themselves grown didactic.'

When I mentioned the Catholic Church, Gilberto threw up his hands. 'Rome is the house of the Pope, and he watches over the University with an eagle eye.' He asked heatedly, 'Do you know that if a boy is caught kissing a girl on the University campus he is suspended? And whose idea is that? The Pope's! We are forbidden to hold discussions on sex. Even the word contraceptive is taboo. Suggestions for plays and exhibitions are submitted to the Board of Censors who decide if they are in line with the thinking of the Church. We are also forbidden to hold any sort of political discussion. The Church takes for granted that most students are good Catholics and since every good Catholic votes for the Catholic Party it sees no point in student politics. The Church takes the same attitude to most of our projects. We are censored at every step.' Then he added solemnly, 'At this University we have no freedom of speech.' I soon saw what he meant. I searched for film societies, for plays, for debates, for discussions, but found none. The only cultural effort was a photographic exhibition.

The Church calls on parents to influence their children's attitude towards sex, work and politics. In Italy this approach meets with much success because, unlike England or America, the young continue to live with their parents after they are twenty-one. I did not know a single Italian girl who shared a flat with other friends, nor a boy under twenty-eight who had his own flat. 'First we must finish the University, then spend two years at military service. And when we begin work we don't earn enough money to set up by ourselves,' a great friend Andy explained. But it is not the whole answer because even the sons of rich parents stay within the family. 'Family life is so restful. It is the only place where you are not cheated, maligned or despised,' said one boy cynically.

The Church has a devastating effect on the upbringing of girls. No Italian girl that I knew could go out alone before she was eighteen, and for several years afterwards lived under meticulous supervision. Though I made many great friends among Italian girls, I often found their behaviour and outlook on life astonishingly old-fashioned. Sex is not even a topic of gossip.

It is hardly mentioned and certainly never at home. One friend told me that when she was sixteen her mother gave her a gramophone record explaining the facts of life. 'She was slightly shocked when I told her that I knew it all already,' she added.

Girls must always be 'correct', no bawdy jokes, no drink except lemonade, and no hugging on the dance floor. Though at times they found it irksome, most of the Italian boys that I knew, those that I met on my second visit, approved of the strict moral attitude among girls. Many said frankly that they wanted to marry a virgin. In Italy chastity matters, and a girl's reputation is still prized. I shall never forget an evening when I lost my key. At three in the morning I sat with Pierre Andrea and Fabio, my greatest friends, in the Piazza Euclide, eating ice creams. We were debating what I should do. Pierre Andrea offered me a room in his flat; his parents were away and there was plenty of room. Fabio dismissed the idea at once. ' She couldn't possibly sleep in your flat. The maid will find her there in the morning and the story might get about, and then so much for her reputation.'

'What other people might think' matters above all in the closely knit *Società Romana*. Rome society is far too static. Composed of poor aristocrats and rich commoners, its rules never waver, nor does it take in any artistic or unconventional newcomers. Most of my friends were in its midst, and they openly confessed to its dullness. 'The young all know each other so well,' Andy sighed, ' I know every girl as well as I know my own sister. I have sat next to them at children's parties when I was three, at fancy dress parties when I was ten, at dinner parties when I was seventeen. Who could flirt with a girl after that!' In their student days my friends found solace with prostitutes under the bridges of Rome, with carefree art students, with *amichetee* in the countryside – village girls who might well have been taken from a Musset play, and with foreign girls on the golden beaches at the famous resorts.

'All the same,' said Alberto, a young painter with a beard and blue eyes, 'sex is quite a problem for Italian boys. After all, you don't want to have to rely on a tart. It took me a long time to realise how extremely moral Italian girls are. When I was fifteen I spent my time going to X films. I lapped up the few passionate love scenes that had passed the censors, but once out of the cinema, in the streets of Rome and in parks or even at parties, no one was doing anything. It was most disappointing. And the effect,' he concluded, ' is that we behave like lunatics at the sight of any foreign girl with less rigid ideas of morality.'

Italian men are famous for amorous ebullience. The police stop traffic when they see a pretty girl and wave her across the street; a bus conductor will hold up a bus, a shopkeeper keep open his door for the sake of an attractive pair of legs. I remember spending some afternoons with Fabio and Pierre Andrea when they had nothing to do. ' Let's chat up a few Americans,' they decided and clambered into their car for a jaunt round Rome. They followed girls for hundreds of yards, whistling and shouting as they drove past. ' We have a lot of energy,' Fabio said simply, ' and nowhere to spend it.'

However, the image of the Italian man as an emotional, romantic and passionate character is far from the truth. My friends were cool-headed, calculating, and at times cynical. But they loved to act. One of my greatest friends, Teddy Belloni, a tall attractive girl with short, curly hair, a delicate face and a wry smile, always maintained that Italian men were inveterate actors. ' All this serenading is put on for foreigners, and the most naïve English and Scandinavian girls fall for it. But in fact Italian men simply don't get carried away. After they come to the end of their string of superlative compliments they sum up the girl in the most dispassionate way.'

' In Rome there is no room for passionate love,' was the sweeping statement made by another great friend, Valeria, a very pretty girl with blonde hair and blue eyes, ' everyone is so concerned with what other people think that they never forget themselves. This may be the country of Romeo and Juliet, but times have changed.' Her opinion was endorsed by Rodolpho, an attractive student of architecture. ' In Italy love doesn't have much elbow room. The moment you take out a girl all Rome thinks you will marry her. Every dishonourable intention becomes honourable under duress and love is swamped by gossip. We are not brave enough. If only we would say hell to the opinion of others, we would become at once less superficial.'

Teddy felt very strongly that life in Rome was superficial. ' Our society is not real. It is based on conventions that no longer

66

mean anything. People won't let their ideas expand with the times. For me Rome is too stuffy; I feel like a woman trying to get into a corset that is too small for her.'

The Church and Roman society frown on the creative arts. It is exceptional to meet a young writer, painter, fashion designer, antique dealer, photographer or journalist. Creative work is associated with the 'decadent' moral standards of England and America. Most university students come from professional families; 'respectable' careers are the natural and often only possibility on the working horizon. The Faculty of Letters provides Italy with most of its teachers, the Faculty of Economics, business men and accountants, the Faculty of Law, lawyers, that of Political Science, civil servants and diplomats. As in France, in choosing your university course you choose your career.

In Roman society girls are discouraged from working altogether. A Neapolitan friend, Anna, whose family has provided Italy with several cardinals, is the most brilliant student I know. She took a degree in Law and throughout her four years of study maintained an average of twenty-eight out of thirty. She then got a part-time job working for a lawyer and is now studying for a degree in Political Science in her spare time. At every step in her academic career she met with family opposition. Her parents thought that university was unnecessary, her grandmother kept saying, 'You will marry one day so what is the point?'

Valeria also was not allowed to work for several years. ' My parents look upon the world as a bed of corruption. Like many of their generation they see no need for a girl to work if she doesn't have to.' She was told to pass the time agreeably until she got married. Parents send their daughters to undemanding language schools or to a course in History of Art. If they are liberal minded their daughters can apply for a secretarial job, but woe if she wants to do something more adventurous! Modelling and acting are put on a level with prostitution.

Teddy often bewailed the retarded outlook of Roman society; 'People live in a world where class distinction and class prejudice flourish, and worst of all, many of the young inherit the prejudices of their parents,' she said. 'You just have to look at their clothes!' Teddy, who loved 'kinky gear', had a point.

At eighteen an Italian girl takes a gigantic stride; from being a schoolgirl she becomes a sophisticated woman. She misses altogether the gay irresponsible spinster years. Suddenly on her eighteenth birthday (usually marked by a wonderful party) she emerges in a knee length black dress with a string of pearls. Her impeccable suits are those of a middle-aged woman; she resembles her mother down to the smallest detail. She would never dream of wearing trousers or a mini-skirt. Instead she is chic, often beautiful, but somehow very old.

'And the men,' Teddy went on, 'they are so unimaginative with their clothes!' Their only interest in their appearance is to be as inconspicuous as possible. Men who wear coloured shirts and garish ties are pansies, and the fear of being mistaken for one drove my friends to sombre extremes. At night they all appeared in dark blue suits, and in the daytime they wore white shirts and dull jackets. They were appalled by my elder brother who came to Rome for a week and turned up at a party in red socks.

At times I missed more than the lack of crazy clothes; I missed a sense of adventure. England rings with the slogan 'the sky is the limit.' In Italy the young seem confined by low hanging clouds. My student friends travelled but, even when they had the money, rarely went beyond Spain or Greece. After university and military service they did not seem to want to explore life, to try out several interesting jobs. They were resigned to a long career in a bank or business planned for them since their earliest childhood.

Upper class Italians conform even in corruption. How often did I hear the remark 'Italy will never change; it will always be corrupt; its vices are a way of life!' One friend admitted candidly, 'We all try to cheat each other, outside the family that is. An Italian's loyalty extends to his family and to his few intimate friends but not beyond.' He told me that during his father's absence from their flat in Rome the servant who was in charge had cheated his father over the food bills. 'My father never found out because I never told him. I didn't want to make trouble. Everyone in Italy cheats their employers and the employers cheat the tax man.'

I knew many Italians in business who kept two account

books, one for the tax man and one for their own use. Most of my friends not only accepted this outlook but found it amusing. They were part of the picture painted by Doctor Barzini in his book *The Italians*, in which he brilliantly analyses modern Italy.

It is the Italian way of life which makes all laws and institutions function effectively. It is the illusion of a solution, lotus eating, the resigned acceptance of the very evils man has tried to defeat, the art of decorating, ennobling them, calling them by different names and living with them.

And yet beneath the surface a spirit of revolt is growing, spearheaded by the young communists. Rome University has a long history of riots and strikes and communist students have been at the centre of each demonstration. In 1966 at the time of elections for the Student Parliament, a communist was killed in a fight. Most people who saw it agreed that the boy's death was an accident; he fell from the steps and hit his head on the concrete. The communists, however, claimed that he had been pushed over the side of the steps by fascists and they barricaded themselves inside several Faculties demanding the resignation of the Rector. He, they argued somewhat perversely, was responsible for the outbreak of violence.

For almost ten days the University was shut; the law did not have the right to intervene in University affairs unless it was at the specific request of the Rector. Police roamed the campus but could do nothing, for the Rector did not give the order to clear the buildings. Inside the Faculties several hundred students crouched on the floors of the lecture halls and slept on desks and in corridors. Food was smuggled in during the night by sympathisers who scaled the walls. 'It was a thrilling experience,' said one, 'like a religious retreat.' After nine days of hesitation the Rector resigned. The doors of the Faculties opened and the triumphant students emerged.

Communist students were the driving force behind another University strike that began soon after I arrived in Rome and extended over the whole country. I attended the inaugural meeting. A television team had set up cameras in the amphitheatre and in the Faculty of Mathematics. By chance I found myself next to one of the organisers, a good looking young man with a black beard, dressed in a dark brown suit and an intense red tie.

'We have tried to argue with the authorities but they and the Government are deaf to every proposal of reform. We must have better university conditions, more grants, more room and more say in university affairs.' Although they supported the communist party few of the students I met seemed dedicated Marxists. Even the bearded young man admitted that he supported the communists only as a protest: 'I dare say that when I have finished university I shall become a bureaucrat like everyone else.'

For the first time this strike had the support of Assistants and Professors. Departments were closed, offices and lecture halls empty. The strike was timed to cut across the biennial examinations, normally held in February. All examinations were postponed. Students crowded round notice boards announcing future dates.

A small number of professors who disagreed with the strike continued to lecture, among them the charming and eminent historian, Valsecchi. I attended his lecture and spoke to him afterwards. 'Italian universities are in a state of crisis,' he acknowledged. 'They have been neglected for too long. But strikes are not the way. They have been tried before with no avail. You will see, nothing will come of this strike,' he added sorrowfully.

Nevertheless the communists were jubilant; in the two weeks that I was in Rome they organised the strike, distributed several thousand leaflets, pinned posters to every bill board and tree on the campus, staged a protest meeting against the suppression of student freedom in the University of Madrid, and marched in a procession denouncing American intervention in Nicaragua. The word communist did not appear on any poster, or even in any speech, for by law all party politics were to be kept out of the University. However, Mario, a charming Assistant in the Faculty of Law, knew several of the agitators and their political colours were no mystery.

'Communist students will take up any cause against the authorities,' Mario told me. As a member of the University Sports Committee he himself owed them a debt. He and his colleagues had fought a long battle with the authorities to gain possession of derelict land just outside the University on which they hoped to build a sports centre. 'At the time the University had no sports centre at all.' He went on, 'We used all the conventional means to press our claims but to no avail. The Government was planning to use the land for blocks of flats. Finally we decided to occupy the ground until the Government changed its mind. We pitched our tents and sleeping bags on the rough site. Many of our supporters were left-wing. They galvanised their friends to help us and, largely due to their support, we got our way.'

All communist students, from the luke-warm to the passionate, were agreed that if Italy went communist it would on no account join the communist block. The world movement had no appeal to Italian individualism. 'Who likes pasta in Russia?' one student asked.

Surprisingly few admitted to atheism. 'You reach a compromise,' one said, 'I confine my religion to the political side of my life.' A science student told me that he would never tell his parents that he supported the communists: 'They would be profoundly shocked. I go to Mass with my family and to Confession, but I don't tell the priest that I am a communist. Since the Church and the communists are intractable it is I who must make the compromise.'

Gilberto and his liberal associates were pressing for reform less violently but with no less determination. 'We will never become educated politically,' he said, 'unless we learn to rely more on argument than on strikes and violence. If you put communists and fascists in the same debating hall there would be open warfare in five minutes.'

The centre of revolt is the Faculty of Architecture, set on a hill in the park Viloa Ruffo. I spent a great deal of time there. My guide, Alfred Cochrane, was conspicuous; he had red hair and freckles and looked permanently amused. Half Irish, half Lebanese, he had been to Eton, lived in Ireland, and had finally taken up residence in Rome in a studio in Via Margutta that was the envy of all his friends. Alfred was carefree, intelligent, and excellent company. He loved architecture and had many student friends.

'The atmosphere is far more personal in this Faculty than in most others because Professors take a real interest in their students,' he told me, as we took our places in a large, modern amphitheatre. A small ugly Professor tramped noisily across the platform and took his seat. Silence fell. The Professor peered through his glasses and began his lecture. He waved his arms, emphasised his words with specific gestures of his hands. He seemed to assume that his lecture was interesting – which it was. He kept his audience alert, and threw out questions.

'Do you understand?' he asked, after he had put forward a debatable opinion. 'No, I don't,' came a voice from the back of the hall. 'Well, come down here to the front,' the Professor said, 'and tell us what it is that you don't understand.' The boy, a Greek, skipped down the gangway and leapt onto the platform. He spoke into the microphone and a long rowdy discussion ensued. The lecture hall acquired the atmosphere of a bull ring.

In the corridors girls with jeans and uncombed hair strolled arm in arm with Italian beatniks. The tone was off-beat and exciting, a far cry from the neat respectability of the main University campus where I had never seen a girl in trousers or a boy without a tie. Alfred, dressed like a bargee in the thirties, found most of the Professors amusing individuals. Many were open communists and wrote for left-wing magazines. Lectures were unpredictable, provocative, and often political. Yet the professors were not lax.

I went with Alfred to a lecture on the science of Greek architecture. A little, fat Professor ran to his desk and began his lecture in a burst of energy. He hardly had time to look at the rows of students in front of him before he poured forth a torrent of questions to which he provided the answers while projections flashed on the screen behind him. Meanwhile I was bombarding Alfred with questions. Suddenly the Professor stopped speaking and stared at me severely over the top of his glasses. In a menacing voice and at great speed he said: 'If you don't stop talking I shall have to ask you to leave the hall. I don't know why you bother to come to my lecture if you are not interested in the subject. Just stay away and leave others to probe the mysteries of architecture. *Dio mio, queste donne*,' and he returned to his subject. Alfred and his friends chuckled at the reprimand. 'He's kinder to girls,' Alfred whispered. 'He'll send a boy out for sneezing.'

After the lecture Alfred continued his graphic description of the volatile Professor. 'He ordered me to leave the room for talking. I wouldn't, and to the stupefaction of the entire hall he thundered from the platform like a Viking on the warpath, puffed up the gangway to where I sat and chased me out of the room, clambering over benches, wheezing past my friends, who were clutching their stomachs with laughter.'

'This is a faculty full of surprises,' Alfred beamed. 'I shall never forget the first lecture. I arrived at five in the evening on a damp day in November. It was already dark. I found my way to the amphitheatre. The porter warned me that the lights wouldn't be turned on until five minutes before the lecture began, and I was early. I stumbled to a seat and sat blinking in the dark, listening to the intense silence. Suddenly the lights went on and to my amazement, dotted throughout the amphitheatre, boys were wrapped round girls, passionately kissing.'

A degree course in architecture lasts several years, and seminars are obligatory. In the spring and summer students go out into the city of Rome and confront the beauties of architecture face to face. Sometimes they amuse themselves by making up stories about particular stones or pillars and telling them to gullible tourists. One afternoon I joined Alfred and his friends at the Colosseum. They were sitting on artists' stools or on car bonnets, drawing an assigned arch. The keen students were forever leaving their seats, or emerging from inside cars to take a closer look at the arch. A boy stood back and measured proportions with his thumb, a girl crouched under the arch to gauge the exact construction of the roof.

A Greek student sat with his drawing pad on his knees. 'Imitators,' he muttered, 'the Romans were just imitators. There's nothing original in this Colosseum. The Greeks evolved the mathematical principles for this pathetic piece of plagiarism thousands of years before Romans were ever heard of.' A storm of protest burst from Italian patriots. But the Greek persisted. 'The Romans never produced any original art. If you want to see great architecture or sculpture go to Athens, go to Greece.' The young Assistant appeared and the argument subsided. He looked at the drawing of a pale Italian girl. 'Are you joking?' he asked her. 'Is that meant to be an arch? And what about the proportions? *Le proporzione*?' Suddenly his attention was caught by a pretty Swedish tourist, who stood in her mini-skirt gazing up at the Colosseum. 'Now those are proportions that even I would like to draw.'

The strongest antidote to communism in the University came from the Young Europeans. They felt that the problems which faced the University were part of the problems that faced Italy, and the solution lay in a federal Europe. Mario introduced me to Eugenio, a thin, blonde haired Italian from Milan, who was an official in the Young European Movement in Rome. Eugenio felt that economic ties in Europe were not enough: 'Though for Italy the Common Market has been marvellous and has greatly helped to reduce poverty, we need the stabilising influence of political ties in order to control the extremists, particularly the communists. They are a real danger; the Church is powerless against them, but in a federal Europe they would be strangled.'

Another staunch European, Guillio, a fat, dark haired boy in his third year of Political Science, felt that only a federation of Europe would solve Italy's endemic problem: disunity. Rome is the centre of the University solar system; students come from all parts of Italy. Neapolitans, Venetians, Milanese sit next to each other in the same lecture halls and in the small seminars. But they regard each other not as compatriots but as foreigners. Southerners despise northerners, northerners pour scorn on the *terrone*, the earthworms of the south. The unification of Italy did not arise out of any surge of national feeling; it was a political move and today the ties that join the different regions are political ties. Ory Coletti, an enchanting friend, studied political economy in Milan. It was the bane of his life for he was a Roman, and he spent most of his time driving along the autostrada del Sole that links the two cities. 'In Milan the people do nothing but work. They don't laugh, they don't enjoy themselves; they think money, they talk money, their eyes reflect money. *Sono antipatici*. In the south people are warm and generous.' Guido, a young business man, was driven mad by the southerners. 'I shall go back to Milan as soon as I can. Here they do nothing. How the city functions God knows. Romans are parasites; they live off the north.'

Apart from the basic conflict between north and south, Italy is divided by an intense rivalry between the cities. Florence hardly feels it worth her while to compete in this beauty contest. She waves her hand imperiously at her art treasures, at the unspoilt beauty of her hills, and calls it a day. Rome can speak for each era of Italian art; she points to the Forum, then to the Bramante Chapel, then to her magnificent Baroque churches. Venice scorns these cities on land; the prize must be hers, for she is unique with her canals, great palaces and Umbrian art. Siena cries out Dante, Naples beckons to the mysteries of Pompeii, and Milan, taking a different line, insists that she is the economic backbone of Italy, that without her these artistic cities would crumble into ruins.

Though most Italians were enthusiastic supporters of the Common Market they did not look upon France as the natural leader of Europe. 'The French don't inspire Italians,' Mario declared, 'each Frenchman has his *folie de grandeur*. So do the English but they believe more in the maxim, live and let live. The French ram their superiority down your throat.' Dislike of de Gaulle was universal. Pierre Andrea made one of his inimitable Italian gestures at the mention of the General. 'He inflates the heads of the French with nothing but hot air.'

The English, so despised in France, are regarded with a mixture of respect and affection. 'What we admire most in the English is what we do not possess, their belief in democracy, their tolerance and their courage,' said a young Professor. Several people spoke of England's role during the war. 'The English fought not only for their own lives but for an ideal,' said a law student. 'Italians are idealists too, but we are not so good at fighting for a cause. Nevertheless, we admire the quality in others.' To my great surprise few students seemed to doubt that if England joined the Common Market she would eclipse France.

In Rome Beatlemania and the mini-skirt had braved the Vatican and penetrated Italian frontiers. Italy was getting 'with it', as the Roman whizz kids, who congregated each Sunday at the Piazza Euclide, testified. Known as the *parioli* because of the district in which they lived, these artistic characters scandalised the orthodox. Girls wore short leather dresses, flower earrings and coloured stockings; boys paraded in butterfly ties and screaming shirts and bell-bottomed trousers. When I had left Rome the new night-club, The Piper, was causing consternation. In a converted cinema, with pop art blazing on the walls, the long haired, spotty, sweaty English group drew a packed house. '*Non è possibile*,' I heard a friend say as he watched the beads of sweat pour from the brow of the lead singer, 'I have never seen anything like it.' Tea dancing at The Piper soon became the rage, but the Vatican saw the red light and banned dancing at such an early hour. The Piper Market, the avant-garde shop with the latest English clothes, survived the counter revolution; though its wares are thought a joke, it is part of the new 'swinging scene'.

My old friends were unanimous in sensing the change which was transforming Rome. Pierre Andrea felt that it was the fifteen to sixteen year olds who were at last asserting their independence. Girls no longer emulated their mothers in the way they dressed; boys refuted the idea that only pansies wore coloured shirts. My most adventurous friends were invading the professional world. Fabio Imperiali, one of the most intelligent and amusing Italians I knew, and scion of an old Italian family, was publishing his first book of short stories. He had a strong face with sad brown eyes; he laughed loudly but talked little. We had sometimes gone to the theatre together; he collected me on his Lambretta, which I then drove four times round the Piazza Navona; he sat petrified on the back. Sometimes we had spent the lunch hour together in the park near the Vatican. He talked at length of Fellini and the importance of his film *Eight and a Half*, of the stories he hoped to write, of family opposition that he knew he could overcome. I saw him seldom but felt I knew him well, and was delighted that he had become what he had hoped : a writer.

To Teddy the change in Italy was most obvious in the press : 'Five years ago you couldn't have found a quarter of the articles that now appear on sex, religion and the Catholic Church.' In the changing, turbulent mood of Rome even the age old traditions of the University were ignored. I had hoped to take part once again in the *Festa della Matricula*, a three day celebration which marks the end of the biennial examinations, but I had to feed on reminiscences. Two years ago I had driven with Fabio to a piazza near the Colosseum where hundreds of students had gathered in their cars. They wore coloured hats that came to an extended point at the front. Some hats were copiously decorated with playing cards, dinky toys, flags, military skeletons, orange peels and banana skins. Cars tore round the city all day confusing motorists. We joined a cavalcade in the Piazza Venetia, and drove in two rows of five cars abreast to the Colosseum, at not more than five miles an hour. Students hung from car windows, twirling rattles and blowing horns and whistles. The rush hour traffic crawled behind us; desperate business men blared their horns and shouted from their windows. We shrieked with laughter. By the time we arrived at the Colosseum the traffic in the Piazza Venetia had come to a standstill. Police on motor bikes flew along the wide streets shaking their fists.

But those days were past. A strike and a protest march took the place of the *Festa*. 'When we sacrifice *la dolce vita* it is serious,' said Pierre Andrea. He put down student violence to the fact that Italy was a young democracy. 'No one is quite sure what democracy means. To whom or to what does the Italian owe his loyalty?' he asked. 'We are looking and questioning; nothing is sacrosanct. Our parents under Mussolini were denied this freedom of thought and find it difficult to understand our restlessness and dissatisfaction. They don't realise that we have thrown down the gauntlet.'

Parents can no longer be in any doubt. In the last few months Rome has been torn by student riots. Police have been hurt, their vans overturned and burnt. It seems that the Mona Lisa is no longer smiling, that the *dolce vita* has turned sour. The cynical conviction that nothing can ever be done to change Italy has been cast aside. It remains to be seen whether violence will bring about university reform where discussion has failed.

The great danger of student violence is that it provides extremists with the ideal opportunity for promoting their own ideas. Communists above all are trying to manipulate the issues to suit their own purposes. The protests of students in Italy today, directed against an apathetic Ministry of Education, might well be the rumblings of a distant volcanic eruption; if the lava rolls no one is sure what will remain, the Church or a red flag.

4

Freiburg
May 1967

My red Mini-Minor had lost the shining aura that radiates from all new cars. It almost looked second-hand. The chequered tape that I had stuck to the doors dangled loosely; the boot hung on one hinge; the back lights were smashed and above the fender a deep dent and chipped paint recalled a painful memory. Poor car, I thought one bright spring day. It was battered but still intact and I was about to take it on its longest journey yet. First I would drive to Paris, to smell the spring in Saint Germain, then east to Freiburg overlooking the Rhine, then on through Frankfurt and East Germany to Berlin. From Berlin I planned to go to Leiden to visit my crazy Dutch cousin who had won yet another beer drinking contest, and then finally head home. With a *mille feuilles* in my hand I climbed into my Mini, waved to Rome and headed north.

In the morning haze the Schwarzwald that surrounds Freiburg has the same dormant beauty as the hills of Tuscany. I arrived in late spring when the beech trees were bursting into leaf, dazzling the stately pines with their piercing green.

Painted wooden houses of the sixteenth century, with high grey slate roofs, and engravings above the windows and doors; a magnificent cathedral smothered in gargoyles; narrow streets of dolls' houses, with balconies and black beams fixed in patterns on the white façades; mosaic roofs; gothic windows; these are some of the famous sights of Freiburg. In 1120 the Herzog Konrad founded the town as a free borough. In 1200 the Herzog decided to build a city wall that would link ten city gates. Today two of the gates and remnants of the medieval wall survive. The Martins Tor is a tall square tower built above an

78

archway. Two turrets are perched beside the remarkable wedge shaped roof. Nearby the sixteenth century Kaufhaus, an old exchange centre embellished with mosaic turrets, stone arches and fighting saints, overlooks the cathedral square that has been a market place for over six hundred years. Flower stalls, wooden stands with vegetables and fruit stand under the shadow of the great cathedral that dwarfs the town and can be seen rising above the slate roofs and narrow streets from the nearby hills.

From where I stayed I could contemplate the town and the cathedral at leisure. The house overlooked Freiburg and the narrow valley in the heart of the Schwarzwald. I was staying with Werner von Simson, a professor at Freiburg and an old friend of my father. Werner has a marvellously expressive face; his eyes are warm with sympathy and understanding. During the thirties he was a violent opponent of Nazism and eventually came to England.

Since my earliest childhood I had heard my parents talk of 'the war' and 'the Germans'. My father spent four years in a prisoner of war camp. Because by nature he is a compassionate man he has spoken little of his feelings for the Germans of the older generation, in case it might prejudice his children. As I crossed the Rhine I was arrested by the thought that for the first time I would meet and talk to people against whom my father and all England had fought with such passion. Suddenly I felt tremendously curious to know the children of these Germans.

Werner took me to the University. It consisted of two main buildings, the old centre of the University the Kollegiengebäude I, now devoted to the Faculties of History and Philosophy, and an ugly new building, the centre for Economics, Political Science and Law. A third building, then incomplete, would house part of the Faculties of Science and Law. Every bare wall, every tree trunk and bill board was covered with an advertisement for a student meeting, a film or a university project taking place that evening. The next morning just as many sheets of paper were pinned to the bill boards and to the barks of trees but they all referred to the events of that same day. I realised that here was a provincial university very unlike Aix.

Fritz, a student of Werner's, kindly offered to show me round. Tall, with long black hair, he wore jeans and a leather jacket and thick black rimmed glasses. In his pocket he carried a copy of Ortega y Gasset's *The Rebellion of the Masses*. We walked through the wide corridors of the University; I was struck by the intense atmosphere, by the serious intelligent faces. Fritz needed someone to help him distribute leaflets outside the *Mensa*, the student restaurant, and I volunteered. In front of the *Mensa*, a dull red brick building, we were joined by members of the student government who provided the leaflets announcing a general meeting of the executive. I was surprised to see such old students; they looked twenty-five or more; they were friendly, but not cheerful. From narrow alleys and side streets the students joined the solemn flow that spilled with joyless resignation into the open doors of the restaurant.

Silent girls carrying bulging satchels walked arm in arm with intellectual beatniks holding Kant and *Der Spiegel*. They hardly raised their eyes as they took the leaflet that I offered. From unflinching faces blue eyes glanced contemptuously at the word *Wichtig* (important) in faint grey print and dropped the leaflet to the ground; men shook their heads as if in despair of the whole human race. Faces didn't lose their character and merge into a blurred, grey, swarming mass; striking expressions kept the picture in focus. I sensed good will but could not shrug off the sadness that seemed to come down from the dark country-side. I noticed such pensive, concerned expressions; everyone seemed immersed in their own thoughts.

Fritz and I distributed leaflets for an hour then sat on the lawn outside the *Mensa*. It was a clear hot day and the lawn was crowded with students lying in the sun. The gardener arrived and set up a rotating hose forcing everyone to the rim of the lawn. 'He always chooses lunch time to water the grass,' Fritz laughed. 'I think I shall try to block off the water,' he said and ran up to the hose. He put his finger over one of the holes; I heard a scream. The water had spurted out with twice the force from the other hole, soaking a girl who sat quietly on the grass reading Goethe.

The sun grew hotter. We talked. Fritz, like all the students I was to meet, wanted to talk about the Second World War. I asked if it was a subject he discussed with his parents. 'Never,' he said sharply, 'it is pointless. They refuse to admit the truth. They try to persuade us that they knew nothing of the atrocities in the concentration camps but we don't believe them. They didn't know because they didn't want to know. We can't understand how they allowed Hitler to rise to such an all powerful position.'

He told me that in the University students of modern history are shown early Nazi propaganda films to help them understand the rise of the Third Reich. The teaching was violently anti-Nazi. 'Almost too one sided,' said a young History don. 'The young are disgusted with their parents' generation,' Werner von Simson told me with conviction. I heard him conduct a seminar. The discussion turned to the ethical problem, do right and wrong exist in the abstract? Professor von Simson told his class, 'All human beings have an innate sense of right and wrong. Those who threw the Jews into the gas ovens knew despite all the Hitler propaganda that what they were doing was wrong.'

Many young Germans I met were plagued with a sense of guilt. They could not and would not let themselves forget and it deeply affected their personal lives. A girl in an empty auditorium, books spread on the desk in front of her, holding a pencil in her hand, told me, 'I cannot help the restlessness I feel when I am with my parents and their friends. Over and over I say to myself, what were you doing in the war, and you and you?' A sub-editor of the University magazine knew the same doubt. 'I am quite unable to talk to my parents about the war,' he said. 'I know my father was sympathetic to the Nazis and unless I want to destroy the entire unity of my family I had better never mention the subject.' He was glad to be at Freiburg. 'It is far from home. I feel more free to think and have time to work out a basis of understanding with my parents. It can never be more than peaceful co-operation.'

Fritz admitted, as we sat drinking the local wine in a café in the cathedral square, that at seventeen he too had rebelled against his parents. 'I couldn't stand being in the same room as them. I refused to speak to their friends, I even tried to run away. I was so ashamed of being German. Gradually you grow more tolerant as you realise that you can't change the past. But you are determined to make up for it in the future.'

The future for German students is at the end of a six or seven year degree course. During that time most students change university at least twice, if not three times. A mobile student population is part of the concept of academic freedom, (*akademische Freiheit*), a reaction against the rigid university programme under Hitler. Academic freedom gives the student the power to choose exactly what he wants to study and for how long. The university term is divided into two halves or semesters. The first semester runs from the end of April to the end of July, the second from the end of October to the end of February. There is no set curriculum. A student who decides to study History can make up his own time-table from a list of over thirty classes posted on boards in the hall of the Faculty of History. At the end of the first semester, when he has had a chance to attend most of the classes which interest him, he must hand in a definitive time-table. The only rule of the university is that students cannot sit their Final Schools in under eight semesters. Examinations, the equivalent of the BA, fall into two categories : the *Staatsexamen* and the *Diplomprüfung*. The *Staatsexamen* leads to a teaching job or to a post-graduate course, the *Diplomprüfung* to business and industry.

Older students contributed much to the academic life of Freiburg through their greater knowledge and intelligent approach to learning. Unlike their counterparts at Aix, they did not stand in awe of their professors. The prevalent attitude was, ' We are here to learn and get as much out of our professors as we possibly can.' In choosing a subject students placed great importance on the character of the professor, particularly since, at the end of each term, they had to sit an examination in the seminar that he had conducted. Since seminars were small the personality of the professor mattered. Many students knew the academic staff quite well.

On the fifth floor of the Kollegiumgebäude II, in the Institute for Foreign and Private Law, I attended a seminar held by Werner von Simson. Two students had volunteered to prepare a short speech on different themes allocated by the professor. The first theme in this top grade seminar (*Oberseminar*) discussed the limitations placed by law upon the freedom of the individual. Thirty students sat round tables all in their middle twenties. They looked thoughtful and sophisticated. When the speech had been delivered a discussion began and the students gave their points of view quite freely. At the end of the two hour seminar that ranged from a discussion of the Kantian philosophy of good and evil to the stand taken by law on matters of conscience, students rose with a sense of achievement. It was the first seminar of the term and Werner invited his class to a pint of beer in one of the open beer cellars where, under the spring sky, the class continued the discussion.

Greatly impressed by such high-powered discussions I was little prepared for the prose seminar that I attended the following day in the old university building, guarded by the statues of Homer and Plato who sit in philosophic positions at the top of the entrance steps. Ten minutes before the lesson began all the seats had been taken and students had no alternative but to sit in the gangways or to stand. I felt in familiar university surroundings. As the professor walked in he looked with surprise at the fifty students who packed the small room. 'Oh dear,' he said with dismay. 'I hoped you would be less. It is so difficult to create an intimate atmosphere with so many of you. However, I cannot exactly throw you out so I had better begin.' I found this an ungracious beginning but other students did not seem to mind. They were mostly in their first year and looked at the professor with bewildered admiration as one might look at a magician.

Clemens Brentano was the subject of the seminar, but the first three quarters of an hour were spent listening to a classic beginning of term lecture. '*Meine Damen und Herren*, university is not a place for irresponsibility and pleasure but a place for study.' 'Good grief,' my neighbour sighed. Painstakingly the professor read out a list of advisable books and added with pride that there was an additional bibliography available containing the names of all well-known bibliographies. At the end of the first half of the lesson morale was not at its peak. In the second half the class was asked to examine a lullaby by Brentano of exactly eight lines. The professor ignored the artistic and literary beauty of the famous poem; instead he concerned himself with its two trochaic inexactitudes and discussed at length whether it was correct to say *singe leise leise leise* with the emphasis on the first, on the second or on the third *leise,* or even, on the *singe.* I was sitting next to a pretty, blonde girl. In a low voice she said, 'It is all very well being interested in detail, but seven years of this and I'll be in a lunatic asylum.'

The girl, Heide, seeing that I was a foreigner, invited me to drink a cup of coffee in the *Mensa*. We sat on the terrace and discussed the University. 'Every course could be cut by a third,' Heide said. 'We learn utterly useless information that we can't use even in examinations.' The Government was in the process of reforming the university system and shortening the courses. 'I do wish they would hurry up. I have at least five years of study, too long when at the end of the road I shall be nothing more than a teacher.' Her older friends grew increasingly restless as the years passed. 'Men of twenty-six just shouldn't be students,' she said emphatically.

Heide knew none of her professors. 'They don't take any notice of first year students. We are just names and numbers. My seminar should consist of twenty students, but, as you saw, over fifty people flood into the classroom.' In her hand she held an edition of the University paper. Every week articles appeared demanding better university conditions. Heide showed me one of the wittier examples. A large printed form covered a page of the magazine. 'Fill up the form and send it to your professor,' ran the editorial.

Dear Sir,
Professor................Lecturer................
During the last winter semester of 1965/66 I attended your lecture................ seminar................ on................
We both hope for a better distribution of the teaching forces at the university and, therefore, I offer the following constructive criticism :

Your subject matter was : ... your doctor's thesis of 1896
                           ... a subject that we have already
                                              studied
                           ... out of date
                           ... pre-cooked
                           ... at last something new

Your method of delivery
                         was : ... trying
                                 ... bearable
                                 ... better than David Frost
                                 ... gripping

You spoke :

... inaudibly
... feebly
... with a lisp
... with a stammer
... fluently

For exam purposes your
lecture is :

... deadly
... a waste of time
... innocuous
... helpful
... indispensable

Your comportment was :

... that of a professor
... that of an actor
... affected
... smooth
... agreeable

On the whole your
lecture was :

... exacting
... insupportable
... informative
... genial
... fascinating

I glanced through the rest of the paper; most of the articles were political. I was not surprised for I knew that politics were the life blood of German students and, like all German universities, Freiburg was caught up in the wave of left-wing thinking. I had not met one young conservative. 'Of course not,' Fritz exclaimed. 'No young German could possibly be right-wing. It smacks of Fascism and the *Hitlerzeit*. Everyone wants to dissociate themselves from the right and the surest way is to join the extreme left. People turn their backs on one extreme to fall into the arms of another. I wonder if the two are very different,' he murmured.

The Communist Party was banned in West Germany so the Marxist students joined with the Socialists in the *Sozialistischer Deutscher Studentenbund* (SDS), affiliated to the national party, the *Sozialdemokratische Partei Deutschland* (SPD). For less extreme Socialists the *Sozialer Hochschulbund* held out its hand. Moderate parties were regarded with suspicion. To left-wing students even the Liberal Party smacked of Fascism, while the Conservative 'Ring' was considered beyond the pale. The Conservative student group had the support of the Catholic and Protestant organisations. These groups were supposedly apolitical, but very few people in Freiburg stood outside politics, least of all the Student Government, *Asta*, which by university law was required to concern itself only with administrative questions. In fact it reflected the strong left-wing trend in German universities. Most of its members belonged to the SDS and saw their role as essentially a political one. The Department of Political Affairs pretended to be an information service but in all debates on Vietnam the anti-America bias was thinly concealed. In administrative affairs the battle raged beween the young left, who felt that the future of Germany lay in their hands, and the conservatives of the older generation, the same conservatives who had led Germany to Nazism.

Werner introduced me to the president of *Asta,* a tall young man of twenty-one with reddish hair and a polite calm manner. He led me to the *Asta* offices directly behind the new university building. We climbed two flights of stairs, passed along a corridor plastered with posters, into the first of three small offices. Four people crowded over a time-table; a secretary typed to the monotonous rhythm of the printing press. The president was addressed as *Herr* by those who did not know him well. He politely showed me into his office where he explained the intricacies of student government.

Asta represented the student interest in the University. It was the link between, on the one hand, the Rector and the academic body, known as the *Akademische Senat,* and, on the other hand, the students. Each province or *Land* had complete control over its university. It elected the *Akademische Senat* from members of its Council and selected a separate body to deal with the university finances. The Senate chose the professors and the Rector and, in most provincial universities, the Rector was subject to the ultimate command of the Burgermeister. To all meetings of the Senate *Asta* had the right to send two of its members. Generally, professors and members of the *Akademische Senat*

86

encouraged the *Asta* president and his colleagues, as part of the post-war move to decentralise German education, to increase the responsibility of students in the management of their university.

Each year elections were held to choose the president of *Asta* and to elect a *Studentenrat,* a parliament of twenty-nine students. Once chosen, the president was free to select his executive, the *Asta,* from the university as a whole. Each one of his executive of twelve was endowed with a department: sport, culture, foreigners, finance, press. The president and some of the higher officials were given a sabbatical year, so that they could devote all their time to university business.

To my delight I arrived at a time of crisis. On my first evening I witnessed a near riot during the first meeting of the *Studentenrat,* held in the largest of the auditoriums, the Auditorium Maximum. The air was explosive; after the long holidays people wanted to see a few sparks fly. The president of the *Studentenrat* was in a cross, pedantic mood. He frowned and scowled as the noise increased, and finally appealed to civilised instincts, a disastrous step. The hall resented his pomposity and burst into whistles and wild shouts, calling for a vote of confidence. The parliament of twenty-eight, excluding the president, divided on the vote fourteen for and fourteen against. In university law equal division meant defeat; to the astonishment of everyone, the student parliament had lost its president.

Internal upheavals were nothing compared with the battle that was raging between *Asta* and the Rector. As soon as it was elected in October *Asta* had put into effect its new reform plan. The first major issue was over the right of the University Tribunal on which Rectors and other members of the *Akademische Senat* presided, to punish students for crimes committed and paid for outside the university. The Rector felt that the present law was justified on the grounds that the university was responsible for its students. All week the photostat machine churned out leaflets with the heading, *Keine doppelte Bestrafung mehr!* (Down with double punishment!) Each day at lunch time new pamphlets were issued announcing the stage that the battle had reached.

On 11 May the student parliament decided to send a petition to the Regional Courts responsible for the laws of the local university, asking for a review of the existing law book. Until word was heard from the Courts *Asta* decided to withdraw its representative from the Tribunal. No university court could convene unless at least two students were present. The president of *Asta* was called to the Rector's office but he held his ground. I saw him often, since *Asta* had become my source of university information. He was making a stand on principle, supported by wildly enthusiastic colleagues, most of whom were carried away by the irresistible idea of suppressed students fighting for their freedom against the tyrannous Rector.

On Tuesday of the critical week news came from West Berlin that the *Asta* at the Free University had won a victory over its Rector. In Freiburg *Asta* students were jubilant. However, tension mounted towards the end of the week as their own feud reached a climax. Whenever I came into the *Asta* offices the printing machines moaned in the background, the telephones rang unanswered, the secretary shouted for help as she typed furiously, ignoring a forlorn newspaper reporter who wanted an interview with the president. Even at this moment of crisis the president and his subordinates showed remarkable coolness and good humour. No matter how busy they were I was always made welcome.

Though I enjoyed the turbulent atmosphere it was refreshing to forget the fight and meet Egbert, who spent most of his days with the Freiburg beatniks sitting by the fountain in the cathedral square playing his guitar. His long blond hair caught the disapproving looks of the passers by. Egbert was a Berliner and he found Freiburg appallingly provincial.

'If you wear any unusual clothes,' (he wore an Indian cape, leather trousers and suede boots) 'the inhabitants think you are mentally unstable.' We sipped the sticky sweet wine in a café by the Kaufhaus. 'The girls here are so ugly,' he went on, 'and those who are not are either Catholic or dedicated virgins.' However, Egbert had found a girl to his taste. She had become pregnant and he had struggled to find the money for an abortion that had taken place earlier in the year. I asked how she was. Egbert stared at the cathedral in front of him with his steel blue eyes and, unperturbed, he answered, '*Sie lebt noch*,' (she is still alive). He laughed when I murmured that he did not seem very concerned. 'Life is your own lookout. Morals and responsibility mean nothing today.'

Egbert rented a room from a landlady in the Sundgauallee, a mile from the University. New residential blocks had been built but many students preferred their freedom. 'My room costs fifty marks a month. I have to go to the floor below to get my running water and I have no heating, but I am independent, and I can have friends in my room. That,' Egbert paused, 'is very important.'

We strolled through the streets. Egbert slung his guitar over his shoulder. In a narrow street behind the cathedral I saw a sign saying 'Carnaby Street'. 'Freiburg is trying to move with the times,' Egbert laughed. Alas, this 'with it' shop, that had hoped to shake the foundations of Freiburg, was struggling to make ends meet. The manageress told us that in the first few weeks business had been excellent; girls felt that it would be daring to wear skirts three or four inches above the knee, but obviously their parents had not agreed because, within a month of opening, the shop was losing money, and it continued to decline. 'Not surprising,' Egbert muttered. 'Freiburg has escaped the mini revolution and will have no trouble with the latest predicted fashions : the 1930s look.'

He was critical of Freiburg in many ways. About one aspect of student life he felt passionately : the *Korporationen*. These were all-male student clubs that date from the revolution of 1848. They are financed by *Alte Herren*, Old Boys, who attend annual dinners, and usually encourage their sons to follow in father's footsteps. 'The Corps foster the worst German instincts Egbert told me. 'The worst Nazis were Corps members. You are taught intolerance, a senseless love of discipline, and worst of all, nationalism.' I had an introduction to a Corps on the Lessingstrasse, a peaceful street with large houses and gardens that overlook the Dresdam Canal. At number fourteen I found the sign *Suevia Corps*. The door was opened and I was greeted by the Vice-President who offered to show me round.

The rooms were large, with oak panellings, but there was an uneasy clinical atmosphere. Everything seemed part of a tradition or enshrined in a law of the Corps. The dining room, with its huge medieval table and high backed medieval chairs, was the setting for ceremonial meals, at which each Corps member was allotted his specific place according to his position in the Corps hierarchy. There were residents of the Corps. Each new-comer to the club had to reside in the Corps building for at least two terms, then for the rest of their studies they were free to use the Corps facilities.

I noticed a pale-faced young man, wearing a yellow and black ribbon across his chest. He stood cowering in a corner before the Vice-President, who stood bolt upright, spick and span and had impeccable manners. I asked why the young man was wearing a ribbon. 'He's a Fox, a *Fuchs,*' the Vice-President told me. The *Fuchs* was the dogsbody. He ran errands, waited at the table, was obliged to carry out every command of the more senior Corps members.

I asked him what it was like being a Fox. In a toneless voice he answered, 'They treat you like the scum of the earth.' This was sinister. He must be biding his time to treat someone else like the scum of the earth, I thought to myself. I can understand this sort of thing in a public school, where authority goes with age. This incorporates a natural respect for older people. But here, in Freiburg among students of the same age, it seemed remote and ludicrous.

To extract himself from the serfdom of life as a *Fuchs,* the young man had to pass an examination at the end of his first term. He was tested in the history of the Corps, in its traditions, its songs and music, and in his ability as a fencer. Corps fencing is no ordinary fencing. The Vice-President and a friend of his very kindly gave me an exhibition. They stood a few feet apart, their legs rooted to the ground, one arm behind their backs. Swords pointed to the sky. A shout rose in the back yard. Sud-denly one of the two brought his sword down four times at the head of his opponent, only the head wasn't there because he, (cleverly I thought), put his padded arm in the way of the shin-ing blade. Both combatants wore protective head gear. It was now the turn of the Vice-President. He did exactly the same thing : four blows on the padded arm of his opponent. This was all beyond me. I asked for an explanation. In a match between different Corps no protective head gear was worn. 'If you're not quick—it all looks much easier than it is—you get cut by your opponent's sword. But however much you are cut, you are not allowed to move until the match is over. Then the Corps doctor patches you up.' A match lasted about half an hour. First the novices, the Foxes fought each other, and then the experts. 'And who wins?' I asked. 'No one wins and no one loses. It's just fun.'

The other fun aspects of Corps life were the twice weekly drinking bouts, obligatory for all members, when it was a duty to get totally and blindly drunk to the pounding rhythm of the club songs. In the spring at Carnival time there was a fancy dress party and a lunch in the river. Tables and chairs were set up in the shallow water and the Corps members sat down, knee deep in water, to their tomato soup. For all sins committed over the week, Tuesday evening was kept aside as confession night. Any transgressions against the Corps statute book, such as driving while drunk, had to be openly confessed before the Corps who then decided on a suitable punishment.

Nothing was exactly wrong with the young men in the Corps. They were charming to me. But I felt totally ill at ease. I couldn't see the point of all this regimentation, nor why anyone would want to join a semi-military club. (Every morning you had to be up at seven for half an hour's fencing practice.) In the Free University in West Berlin one of the first votes taken by the students was to abolish all *Korporationen* in the university.

'There are three in Freiburg, and I would abolish all of them,' Egbert told me with vehemence.

On Friday evening Freiburg breathed deeply as most of the student population left, some to spend the weekend in the Black Forest, some to drive along the Rhine towards the famous University of Heidelberg, some to visit their parents. For those who stayed at the university the inns in the beautiful old villages with their German Gothic churches, sixteenth century Town Halls and colourful, tranquil countryside provided diversions away from the old town. In the hot summer the Tannesee, a lake that lies deep in the Black Forest not far from Freiburg, swarmed with body worshippers who lay in rows on the water's edge, patiently waiting for the sun to bake their white skins. In the winter and early spring a skiing station on the highest of the nearby peaks drew students and local inhabitants from miles around.

Wherever I was, in the silence of the Schwarzwald, in over-crowded cafés, in the *Mensa*, I listened to passionate discussions about the future of Germany. 'Germany isn't even ours,' said a quiet girl as we sat on a green bench near the *Mensa* lawn. 'It's been pawned and we want to buy it back.' The challenge was great; in a divided country that had lost its capital the young had a past to live down and a future to build up. Kurt, a blond medical student and a former member of *Asta,* spoke at length of the aspirations of his generation. ' We want to regain for Germany her political rights, to feel that she belongs to us and not to the American and British soldiers. Most important of all we want to give her what she has lost, the respect of the world.'

5

Berlin
May 1967 (Part I)

FROM Freiburg I drove along the autobahn to Frankfurt where I spent three days with friends in a suburb, Eschborn am Taunus. On a Tuesday morning at eleven o'clock I put my two suitcases into my red Mini, filled up the car with petrol, turned my radio to a cheery French station and started on my trip to Berlin. I left the autoroute at Göttingen to look at the famous university town. As I was sitting in a café drinking coffee my thoughts turned to a subject which engrossed me so completely that I never moved out of my chair.

It occurred to me that in two hours I would be crossing the border into a communist country. My friends at Eschborn had warned me to leave all controversial books, newspapers, small cameras and anything remotely political behind. They gave graphic accounts of the occasions on which they had been searched at the border, of the grim waiting room where they sat biting their nails, not knowing what would happen, of sour faced guards who seemed determined to find some evidence to prove that they were either smugglers or spies.

Thoughts and words flashed through my mind as I stared into the brown coffee. I remembered newspaper headlines announcing that students had been detained at the border for possessing microfilm. I had laughed and assured my German friends that I had nothing controversial, but in truth I had never given my belongings a thought. I had flung them in the car and with eternal optimism driven off. Suddenly I found myself thinking, 'If I were searched what would they find?'. The list warranted a ten year sentence in Siberia. I had piles of political leaflets from Paris and Freiburg, type-written notes on student politics,

93

newspapers, leaflets, even Russian short stories and textbooks that had once been the basis of spasmodic studies in Aix. I opened my bag to find my Minolta, a six inch Japanese camera with a film only half an inch wide. But the most incriminating material (I could already see the newspaper story – English girl appears in East Berlin on spy charge) was a present from the mother of a French friend. When I had told her that I was learning Russian she had given me a copy of a wartime Russian dictionary of colloquial expressions; it had belonged to her husband, an English civil servant. It was an old book with dark brown patches on the cover that failed, however, to conceal the heavy black print 'War Office, 1940', followed by a mysterious sequence of four letters and three numbers.

I climbed into my car, my hands trembling on the wheel. On calmer reflection I decided to leave all suspect material at the Left Luggage Department in Brunswick Station. Feeling like Mata Hari I carried a bulging duffle bag to the Left Luggage counter; involuntarily I looked over my shoulder half expecting to meet the cold stare of a man in a dark raincoat with a hat pulled over his face. With the Left Luggage ticket in my hand (I hid it meticulously in the lining of the seat), I headed for Helmstadt with much relief.

For all my painstaking efforts the young guard at the border gave my car a cursory glance and pointed to the control office where I spent half an hour filling in forms, declaring currency and paying a road tax. A young guard in his early twenties checked my passport. His colleagues looked as young as he and appeared equally bored. A high look-out tower rose above the final checkpoint. An armed guard faced towards the car park where West Germans waited for their papers to be cleared. Several cars had been opened and luggage taken out and searched. East German cars with their yellow number plates, battered and at least ten years old, contrasted absurdly with the expensive new Mercedes that flowed past the checkpoint to the evident envy of the guards.

The autoroute to Berlin had not been renovated since the days when it was built by Hitler. There was no question of exceeding the seventy kilometre an hour speed limit. Few cars could have gone faster over the pot holes and uneven surface without breaking a back axle. After half an hour of monotonous driving, past flat green countryside, into the increasing darkness of evening the car in front of me was flagged down by a heavy policeman, dressed in black leather, whose motor bike lay abandoned in the lay-by. I too was stopped and during the next twenty minutes the thin but steady stream of cars heading for West Berlin joined the mysterious queue.

No one knew or cared what we were waiting for. I had other problems. The car in front of me revealed four fat East German men who approached and pointed to my car. At once I knew. A flat tyre. What luck though! In five minutes the East Germans had helped me put on my spare tyre. I said practically nothing and at once they presumed that I couldn't speak German. 'Nice car,' one said. 'Wouldn't mind a swop.' 'I wouldn't mind swopping her for my wife,' said another. 'Nifty gadget,' another muttered, looking at the Mini-Minor jack, an ingenious invention for the female driver. With beams of '*Auf Wiedersehen*' they clambered into their pre-war car. A gigantic trailer carrying a tank came grinding along the autobahn on the left side of the road. Twenty yards before it reached the queue of traffic it turned and crossed the autobahn to the other side of the road. Engines sputtered and gears grated, and the long train of cars and transport trucks resumed the journey.

The flicker of lights gave way to the cutting shafts from headlamps as the dull daylight faded to a duller stone grey that drifts over the sky at the end of a lifeless, spring day. Arable land lay in stillness dotted with copses of dark green trees. Black signs denouncing Western tyranny added gloom to the deserted countryside. *Berlin, Hauptstadt der Republik* loomed large on posters. West Berlin was marked only twice and in the darkness it was easy to miss.

I followed a yellow vintage sports car, with a West Berlin number plate, in the hope that the driver was going home. He was, as he told me himself when, at ten o'clock in the evening, we came to the checkpoint into West Berlin. 'You are lost,' said the young man beaming. His mop of yellowish hair half covered his brown eyes. 'Don't worry, we have re-entered civilisation.' We exchanged addresses and he, Hans, offered to guide me to the Kantstrasse where I was staying with a cousin of Irina von Arnim, a young girl Bettina Baehr who was married to a painter.

At the checkpoint a path over twenty feet wide had been

cleared through the forest as far as the eye could see. The tall pine trees stood out against the dying light. A high barbed-wire fence ran through the middle of the clearing, flanked on either side by ten feet of exposed terrain. In pine wood watch towers armed guards with shining boots surveyed the long lines of cars that collected before the red and white barriers, which fell in front of each car in turn. Guards walked in groups, straight backed in their stiff uniforms, watching the West Berliners drive off into the island of capitalism. I did not realise how tense I felt until I saw the British and American flags side by side, and until I heard 'Welcome to Berlin' in an unmistakably English accent. Involuntarily I smiled and the smile was with me all along the twelve kilometre autobahn, smooth and fast as a billiard table, through the parks and woods that surrounded this unparalleled city in Western Europe.

My eyes darted from the dazzling bright lights that danced and gleamed on my windscreen through the rain to wide streets and tall buildings. The door of Number 47, Kantstrasse was locked so I telephoned in a bar. The gentle voice welcomed me to Berlin. I crossed the street and waited under the portico for the door to open; it was raining monotonously. I had long formed an image of Bettina. She would be a plump, homely German *Hausfrau,* respectable, conventional and kind. I pictured her husband as an industrious, slightly humourless artist, who painted fashionable portraits and came home to heavy dinners provided by their South German cook.

A beam of light slipped beneath the door and lit the wet stone steps. Light footsteps descended an unseen staircase and approached; a key turned, the door opened, and Bettina stepped into the rain. Though twenty-four she looked eighteen. Tall, almost five foot ten, and very thin, she wore brown corduroy trousers caked with paint and a man's shirt. Her hair was cropped short like a boy's; she had a beautiful face, thin sallow cheeks, a clear olive skin and enormous green eyes. I was struck by her voice which was unusually soft and by her long, thin, expressive hands.

Ulrich, her husband, was sitting in a high backed chair in the main room of the flat. He was a tall man, strongly built, with brown hair and a thin reddish moustache. East German guards always detained him at the border because they thought he had a suspicious face. We talked together while Bettina insisted on fetching some food.

I stared at my surroundings: furniture made no impression in the high, long room; a feeling of space and expansion spread to all four walls. Ulrich's chair and the blue divan on which I was sitting and two stools submerged in newspapers completed the sitting part of the room. Underneath one of the windows, untrammelled by curtains, was a small table and three chairs. Home-made wooden bookcases lined one wall, bending noticeably under the weight of heavy volumes that spilled onto the bare wooden floor in crooked piles. At the opposite end of the long room stood an improvised full-length ping pong table overshadowed by one of Ulrich's vast paintings. From all sides paintings glared at you – larger than life faces of Churchill, Stalin, Roosevelt and Hitler, painted in pale, anaemic colours.

Ulrich asked me hopefully if I found his style *kitschig,* corny with a touch of chocolate box sugariness. I nodded and he seemed pleased. He never analysed his work. ' Only a bad painter explains with words what he has failed to say on canvas.' The paintings were interesting; I had been told that Ulrich was regarded by art critics as one of the most promising young painters. He seemed to be probing the aura of the super-human war hero. In his work room at the far end of the flat the floor was smothered in newspapers and copies of *Paris Match* and *Der Spiegel.* Blotches of paint coated the walls; rags, brushes, tubes of oils and bottles of turpentine stood on a table made out of a plank of wood and two fruit boxes within an arm's length of a large easel.

Bettina was an engraver. She stamped her own prints on the old printing press in her studio, which was separated from the main room of the flat by a glass partition. Her work room was littered with metal squares, with iron pipes and bottles of chemicals, and newspaper cuttings of space capsules: Bettina was a space age artist with a passion for science fiction. She concocted complicated designs of the interiors of rockets and of the intricacies of space machinery; tubes, bubbles and circles intertwined in her black and white and coloured prints. ' I love to mix this age of mechanics with a touch of imaginary detail,' she told me. Her engravings sold well. 'Anyone who buys my prints must share my sense of humour. My work has only one point, *Es macht Spass*' (It's fun). She laughed.

'Great fun,' Ulrich muttered, 'great, great fun.' It was twelve o'clock on a Sunday morning and we were about to devour the enormous breakfast that he had bought from the market. Ulrich sat in front of the table scowling and then he began to laugh. There were no knives on the table, no butter, no bread. Bettina was no housewife. The milk boiled over while she lay on the floor cutting her new design for a space suit, oblivious to Grace Kelly, the long haired dachshund, who was absorbed in chewing the furniture. The weekly wash was postponed because she had forgotten to turn on the hot water; the flat was seldom swept though it always seemed clean. 'Newspapers keep out dust,' Bettina maintained with some justification. With no curtains she didn't mind dust on the windows. 'It's quite convenient. When the windows are clean Ulrich's pictures can be seen from the street, and several times pedestrians have called the police to check that this flat is not some fascist headquarters.'

My room, like all the rooms in the flat, was big and empty except for an army bed, two chairs, and a plank of wood supported by two empty oil drums that served as a desk. I loved the space; I could jump or skip and turn cartwheels and forget that I lived in the middle of a population explosion. Both Bettina and Ulrich felt the necessity of space. However, in order to pay the rent, they lived, in their own words, on the bread-line. one room was occupied by a lodger, an enigmatic night nurse whom they never saw. 'We just manage to scrape enough money together to buy food and pay the rent. But money isn't really a problem. We don't have any, that's all,' Bettina mused one evening.

She taught in a school during the day. 'I am no good at keeping discipline,' she admitted. 'I try to humour my students into doing what I want, but I never shout as the sound of my own voice makes me laugh.' In the evening she worked at her engraving while Ulrich, locked in his room, painted to the rhythm of the radio. Soon after midnight they stopped work and sat down to a night-cap of beer by candlelight. I looked forward enormously to these late night meetings when we talked and laughed sometimes until the hint of dawn came through the windows. I felt that Bettina and Ulrich and I were real friends; their kindness and ungrudging outlook on life made a deeper impression on me than anything I had experienced all year.

West Berlin is a strange, tenuous city. Parks and wide streets, little noise and no traffic problems create an unusually peaceful atmosphere. In his yellow car Hans took me for a drive through the Grünewald Forest, past the lakes and fields which stretch for several miles to the barbed wire border fences. High above the trees Le Corbusier's communal centre sits like an Etruscan tomb in impressive isolation. We sat in an open café overlooking a bay bright with coloured boat-houses; picnickers crowded the woods; white sails floated on the blue water of the Wannsee; middle-aged couples danced to the music of an Austrian accordion player. 'This might be pre-war Berlin,' Hans whispered.

However, in the centre of West Berlin there is little that evokes the past : a palace perhaps, the Reichstag, the Bismarck Allee, the widest street in the Western sector on which Kaiser Wilhelm I planted his victory column, the Brandenburg Gate, a bombed site or ruined church. But these monuments make little impression on the horizon of the new gleaming city, patrolled by fast Mercedes, infused with expensive shops and open air cafés, and surfeited with spectacular modern architecture. I stood in blue grass in the forecourt of a bank and studied in bewilderment, tortuous iron creations of weaving pipes; I felt the cool spray of an exotic fountain that sprouted narrow shafts of water in geometrical patterns in front of a towering office block. In the heart of West Berlin, high above the garish, noisy street of the *Kurfürstendamm*, shimmers the *Europazentrum*, a modern match box building of shining glass. Inside I discovered office flats, plush carpets, expensive boutiques and display centres, a roof restaurant and at the very top of the skyscraper, beneath the clear summer sky, a spectacular view over Berlin. To the west I saw forests and lakes, to the east enigmatic rows of brown roofs. Directly below me I gazed on to the ruin of the Memorial Church. Today a new *Gedächtnis Kirche* envelops the ruin. Inside the circular stone building irregular slabs of coloured glass let in a strange, subdued light, predominantly deep blue.

At the Brandenburg Gate I felt the drama and brutality of Berlin converge. The Gate stands a few hundred yards behind the Berlin Wall and the lines of barbed wire fences and watch towers manned by East German guards with machine guns.

The flag of the East German Republic flew from the gate flanked by two red banners. West German guards faced the famous street, *Unter den Linden,* that used to be the centre of old Berlin. I stood close to the police barriers and read giant signs forbidding pedestrians to approach. No man's land stretched ahead to the high brick wall. Behind it lay the East. An old man stood beside me. 'The people who live across the wall, they are just the same as us,' he muttered, 'they are all Germans.'

The younger Germans whom I met shared a different attitude. Ulrich told me that many of his friends thought of the Wall only when they read about it in newspapers. The West German Government did not recognise the East and the only means of communication was by post. 'Locked in this island it is so easy to forget the Wall,' Ulrich said as he sat in his high backed chair. It was late in the night. I had arrived clutching beer bottles to add to the night-cap. By candlelight we drank and talked, inevitably of the East. The confrontation of power was foremost in my mind; I was acutely aware of the presence of arms, of the Wall itself, and of the sub-conscious tension that it created. Bettina could not go to the East for she had a West Berlin passport. Ulrich, however, with a West German passport – an important distinction – was free to cross the border.

'It is a sad country, sad for us because we have relations and friends there.' He had visited the Dresden School of Art a few months before. 'As an artist you are trained to paint portraits and copy photographs. Occasionally you design a happy family scene for a propaganda poster. Faces must suit a caption like "Bliss in the DDR", the task of the painter is to capture the look of ecstasy. I had a friend there whose paintings did not conform; he persisted in his individual technique. He was asked to change his style and when he refused he found himself unemployed.'

Both Ulrich and Bettina loathed the Ulbricht regime. 'One can have nothing but contempt for that man, a pawn in the hands of twenty Russian Divisions. He is hated as much inside the DDR as outside,' Ulrich insisted. He knew because his cousin studied Theology at an East German University. 'He is not devout,' Ulrich exclaimed, ' nor fascinated by his subject, but he chose it because he felt that as a theologian he would be of the least possible use to the DDR.'

I knew that Bettina had been brought up in the East. Her father had died a Russian prisoner of war inside Siberia. She seldom spoke of East Germany. 'It is a soul destroying system,' she said quietly. I thought of her cousin Jan, a brother of Irina and Marina von Arnim, who had helped organise an escape route through the sewers into the West soon after the Wall was built. He had been a student at the time. In his house on the edge of West Berlin I met him, tall and strikingly good looking, with his beautiful wife and two small children.

'It was a game at the time,' he admitted. 'We got over seventy students out of the East, and risked being shot. A dangerous game, but a game.' Jan felt that the days of escape from the East were over. The security precautions were, at the present time, too thorough and extensive. The division between East and West Berlin was complete and permanent. Jan saw no hope of the re-unification of Germany. A federation was conceivable, but, as Hans bluntly stated, 'Bismarck's work is undone, and that's all there is to it.' To Hans re-unification was a dead letter that survived only in the minds of some of the older generation and among certain politicians who knew that it aroused much support in elections. 'It is a pipe dream,' he said, 'and most people know it.'

Hans often went over to the East with his friends from the *Technische Hochschule,* one of the two universities in West Berlin. Usually they went to the theatre. The standard of acting was, according to many people, higher than in the West and methods of production were interesting and original. There was also a world famous museum and good art galleries. 'I like to visit East Berlin,' Hans explained, 'as long as I can remain an uninvolved spectator.'

I longed to be a spectator myself, and was delighted when Hans invited me to a play at the *Brecht Theater,* the famous East Berlin theatre. He left his car in West Berlin; to take a car into East Berlin was a highly complicated operation. Foreigners could pass into East Berlin only through Checkpoint Charlie, while West Germans were admitted only by another checkpoint, and West Germans with cars by yet another checkpoint. 'Therefore,' he added with a smile, 'it is simpler to take the train.'

We took the *S Bahn*, an above-ground tube running from East to West and West to East. I peered from the window of the train, trying to memorise every building and street that I saw. We passed rows of the low, black houses that had once covered the city. From a distance I saw the Brandenburg Gate and then the Reichstag, a sombre, gargantuan palace where Hitler had lived. The train stopped and started; passengers filed through the doors, others stepped into the compartment and sat expressionless in their seats. I looked out and this time saw the back of the Brandenburg Gate, but this time I viewed it from the other side; we were in East Berlin. The glare of the big city and the grind of traffic and the evening crowds had disappeared. In their place lay rows of small, dirty houses and an occasional bomb site lit by an isolated street-lamp.

We got out of the train at the first stop. High on the station rampart I saw the silhouette of a guard standing astride holding a machine gun. His orders were to shoot at any figure that made a run for the train heading to the West. Exits were marked for foreigners and for Germans. My passport was carefully examined by a young guard, who handed me a form. I declared what German currency I had, was handed a copy of my statement, and warned that any West German marks I spent had to be accounted for by receipts or bills. I was required to change five West German marks for East German marks and, with a suspicious look, the guard let me through the barrier. I emerged into the street where Hans was waiting for me.

I stood still on the pavement to absorb my first impression of East Berlin. We were in the centre of the city and it was Saturday night. The wide street was lit by faint street-lamps. A few couples strolled along the pavement arm in arm, an old Mercedes rattled by. Neither the sound of footsteps, voices, nor the drone of traffic disturbed the evening air. No glaring cinema lights besieged the eyes apart from the pleading sign, *Bahnhof*, in red neon lighting. As we left the main street and walked towards the theatre, noise ceased. Deep rays of sunset caught no colour in their fading light but fell on grey houses, on ruins and bomb sites, on grey clothes, grey cars and grey water in the river.

The *Brecht Theater* was full. Soldiers queued outside the entrance. 'They are given cheap tickets,' Hans told me, 'so are the workmen in many factories. Only workmen don't have to go while the soldiers do.' We decided to go to the *Maxim Gorki Theater* to see Anouilh's play about Joan of Arc. The production was simple; characters wore ordinary dress, and stools and benches constituted the scenery. The standard of acting was exceptionally high. In the first act of the play Joan made the remark that men in power are not always very intelligent. Quite suddenly all around us the audience began to clap. Hans was not surprised. ' At the *Brecht Theater* this happens all the time. It is one of the few occasions on which East Berliners can express their discontent.'

When we came out, soon after ten, even the old Mercedes that had rumbled along the streets were no longer to be heard. In a drab café by the station where life in East Berlin was at its gayest, we ate a snack with what remained of our East German money. The menu was in German, French, Russian and English. I read incomprehensible suggestions such as 'raw minced meat or pork with egg yolk '.

An hour later we were walking towards the entrance of the railway station when my friend suddenly stopped and went over to the nearest telephone box and felt along the top ledge. ' You are not allowed to take back to the West any East German marks,' he explained. ' But sometimes when I don't want to spend the money I have changed, I hide it here.' He looked disappointed; someone had discovered his hiding place.

As we walked down the station steps, through what is locally known as the ' gateway to Hell ' because of the blinding white lights and the glaring propaganda notices above the entrance, it occurred to us that we had no East German money left for the train tickets. The change desk was shut. East Germans were not allowed to accept West German money since the penalty for harbouring foreign currency of any sort was a jail sentence. (Certain restaurants and hotels had special permission to accept foreign money but by law they had to hand it over to the authorities.) Hans, however, seemed unperturbed. He explained our predicament to the young man behind the ticket desk. ' We can't buy the tickets with West German money can we?' he asked. The young man shook his head. He looked nineteen or twenty. With a curious expression on his face he half smiled at Hans, glanced at the station guard who was deep in a newspaper, and whispered, ' Just give me a cigarette and you can have your tickets.' Surreptitiously Hans passed four cigarettes beneath the counter and we left the desk each with our return ticket.

Three days later I decided to go back into East Berlin to see the city in the daytime. I had been given the name of a professor at the Humboldt University. I left my car in a car park near Checkpoint Charlie on a street that looked like a stage prop for a shanty town : cafés with broken signs, low, battered houses, Charlie's Café, Charlie's Bar, overturned dustbins, dogs prowling among the litter. At the British Passport Office near the barrier a woman asked if I wanted to register. ' You don't have to if you don't want to,' she added quickly. I glanced at the book and decided to sign. It was a comforting thought to know that if I did not come back at least I would not be forgotten.

I walked through no man's land, past the barriers and beneath the high look-out boxes that gave a full view over the Wall. I filled in forms and showed my passport and was told that if I walked for ten blocks I would come to the main street of East Berlin, *Unter den Linden*. I walked the length of the Friedrichstrasse; the city seemed still and deserted. Small stationers' shops stooped between blank houses. I passed the ruin of a French-German church. Through the side streets I could see endless bomb sites and half demolished buildings. I drew closer to *Unter den Linden*, the centre of East Berlin. Expensive shops and restaurants had looked on to the rows of lime trees which stood on the wide pavements on both sides of the street. The chestnut trees were in blossom. Offices had replaced shops. Groups of tourists and school children strolled under the trees, showing little interest in the giant signs that spread along bare walls, announcing that ' The Russian State, the most powerful in the world, brings freedom and happiness to her people'. Another read, ' The Russian State loves her brothers the DDR '. On the other side of the Wall almost facing the Brandenburg Gate the Reichstag flew the West German flag, so that no one who looked towards the Brandenburg Gate could fail to see the rival banner.

At the entrance to the Humboldt University a statue of William Humboldt himself greeted the students. There was nothing modern about the interior of the University. In the drab main hall notice boards announced party meetings, sporting events and political discussions protesting against American imperialism. Students with briefcases filed into classrooms, clutching books beneath their arms. Officially I was not allowed to pass the porter's office without a student card, but the porter raised no objection when I asked to go to the lavatory. On my return I deviated from the bidden route and glanced into classrooms and along corridors. I saw only drabness and dirt. On my return the porter informed me that the professor I was looking for lived in another building. On my way out of the University I passed a giant picture of a radiant young couple smiling ecstatically in an easterly direction. I thought of Ulrich's visit to Dresden. Below the picture a caption read 'The Socialist State brings happiness and hope.'

Off the main street the air was still in the hot sun. A policeman stood languidly on a corner; a woman walked along the street beneath the shadow cast by the ruin of a bombed church; occasionally a tram rattled past. The new buildings and office blocks that look so magnificent on posters lost all their glamour when seen in context, standing next to rows of squalid houses above dirty streets. I asked the policeman for directions. 'The house you want is the next one down the street,' he said pointing towards a wide road. The next house along the street was more than two hundred yards away, past depressing grey bomb sites.

The professor I went to visit worked in the Department for *Hochschulpolitik* that dealt with all political matters concerning the University. He gave me a long talk on the merits of the East German university system, on the variety of subjects it offered, and on the willingness of students to choose their subjects according to the national need. I found our conversation horribly depressing. He spoke of people only in terms of numbers and their mass contribution. I was immensely relieved at five o'clock to leave East Berlin. Men and women – the women whose absence I had felt all day in the stillness of the city – walked together along the Friedrichstrasse towards the main street. I bought a newspaper from a stall that sold only Party magazines. The Western press was forbidden. I read the crude headlines denouncing Western capitalism as I made my way towards Checkpoint Charlie. I felt sick from the claustrophobic atmosphere, from the drabness, the poverty, the lifelessness.

I had seen nothing of the promised happiness and hope. Everything was a lie; each human being was being forced into a mould that was not his own because a few individuals liked the idea of the final shape.

Back in the West I had a long conversation with Karl Senoner, a thin, black haired man of twenty-eight who had grown up in East Berlin and spent two years at the Humboldt University. In 1959 he had left his entire family and crossed the border into the West. He had given several lectures on university conditions in the East and on methods of Communist indoctrination in schools. At the Humboldt University Karl had been a rebel.

'In the East the University automatically assumes that you are a Communist,' he told me. 'In lectures you hear constantly that the truth of Marx is self-evident to all intelligent students. My professors were very worried that I would not accept the Communist doctrine. They told my friends that it was their duty to lead me to the truth of Communism, and I was amazed that many of my contemporaries made a serious attempt.' Karl argued incessantly with his professors. He bombarded them with questions concerning the travel restrictions. One professor explained that the Berlin Wall was being built to defend the freedom of the young. If they travelled over to the West where the Communist Party was banned, they would be regarded as Communists and thrown into prison. Equally, if they returned to the East, they would be taken as spies and also thrown into prison. Therefore it was in their own interests to confine their travel to East European countries.

'I courted expulsion,' Karl admitted. 'I so enraged one professor that he burst out, " It's quite simple; either you are with us or against us ". I replied that this was an absurd alternative. My classmates whispered to me that I had gone too far. For several days I wondered if I would be thrown out, but I received no summons.' Karl knew that his professors felt it more important to save his soul than to give him to the devil. In a violent argument over the restrictions of personal freedom in the DDR Karl imprudently burst out with the comment, ' This country is governed by a dictatorship.' (A blasphemy for which any student would be expelled.) 'I watched the horror on the face of my professor and sarcastically added, " Of the proletariat ", and walked out of the room.'

Karl had left the East because he saw the decay that Communism bred. He watched hypocrisy flourish among his friends. 'Life is based on a lie,' he told me, 'a lie that leads to success.' As part of an experiment Karl wrote an examination paper extolling the merits of Marxist philosophy. ' My professors knew exactly what I thought of Marx, and they knew that I did not believe one word that I had written. I had not fooled them but nevertheless they gave me a high mark in my exam because I had written what they wanted to hear.'

Karl emphasised that young East Germans, though disenchanted with the present system of Communism, had been deeply affected by Communist doctrine. ' If they were all free tomorrow, they would not at once rush into the arms of West Berlin but rather try to set up in East Germany a new type of socialist society.'

In the early days of the Russian regime many Germans, particularly ambitious politicians and professors, had believed in the new system. In the mood of extreme optimism soon after the war East German Communists calculated that in twenty years time East Berlin would be rich enough to provide free transport. Since private cars would almost certainly be obsolete they built the *Stalinallee* with no underground garages. Ironically, their calculations had been almost correct; private cars were practically obsolete.

The gulf between the standard of living in the East and the West was enormous as I learned when I went to visit an old lady, Frau Leider, on the outskirts of West Berlin. She had looked after my flat mate in Aix, Anne, when she had lived in Berlin. Frau Leider had been a refugee from the East. The West German Government had provided her with a generous pension of forty pounds a month. She lived in a neat, modern flat and was able to lead a comfortable life. Staying with her for a few days was an elderly lady, a friend of hers who lived in East Berlin.

' Old people have every chance to " flee ",' she said cynically. ' Each year women of over sixty and men of over sixty-five are allowed to spend twenty-eight days in the West staying with relations. The East German Government would be glad to get rid of us. We are too old to work and they have to pay us a pension, though it is a pittance.' She was given just over twelve pounds a month of which she paid forty marks on rent. She was left with a total of eight pounds on which she was expected to live. 'I would starve if my two children did not help to support me,' she said. Though many of her old friends had left for the West she would never leave because of her children.

Frau Leider was at a complete loss to understand the students at the Free University. 'What do they mean with all their communist slogans? Do they know what it is like?' I could not answer. The university term had only just begun and I planned to visit the Free University the following day. However, I was sure that even if students did realise the appalling living conditions in the East, it made no difference. Their idealism was not likely to be destroyed through other people's experience. ' I still think they are mad,' Frau Leider burst out. ' Probably paid by the East,' she muttered. I had heard this remark from several older West Berliners. I was more than curious to meet these students who were such a mystery to their parents' generation.

6

Berlin

May 1967 (Part II)

THE beer tasted deliciously cool in the midday sun. I was sitting on the terrace of the Student Restaurant at the Free University of West Berlin. Beside me sat Götz Schuffelhauer, a young man of medium height with a round, kind face and short cropped hair. Götz was the Vice-President of the Young European Movement in West Berlin and was well known to my friends at Aix. The terrace looked on to the campus. In the peaceful suburb of Dahlem, low glass buildings spread over the green lawns; stone paths weaved through gardens and trees; large window panes glinted in the sun. Bodies lay motionless on the grass, drinking in the summer heat.

The faculties might have been modern hospital wings; I knew them well for I had spent several days on the campus. The Faculties of Law and Medicine, of Economics, the Institute of Political Science, all lay before me in gleaming glass and metal. The Faculty of Philosophy, a nineteenth century building, squatted uneasily in the modern surroundings. At the far end of the green lawns stretched the high, perpendicular Henry Ford building, in white stone, striped with long, thin strips of glass. It had been built in the same spirit as the Falmer building at Sussex University. Inside I had discovered enormous lecture halls, including the Auditorium Maximum, open to any professor who could claim a large audience. It also contained the University library, a canteen that looked like a British Rail refreshment bar, and the John F. Kennedy Institute for the promotion of American good will.

The whole of the FU, as it was called, was built with American money donated by the State Department and by the Henry

Ford Foundation. The State Department continued to give large sums of money: both the new psychiatric clinic for students at Steglitz and the Chemistry and Science Faculties, under construction near the Dahlem Museum, were being financed by the Americans. On the walls of the Kennedy Institute attractive, alluring photographs of new universities wooed the German students. I was delighted to see that England was not altogether ruled out as a conceivable patron of the English language. Unrecognisable eighteenth century prints of Oxford were grouped on a wall alongside uninspiring notices of summer schools and exchange programmes. America, however, was the first choice of most students. A girl in her fourth year of history who sat reading *Time* magazine explained, 'We are restless, always looking for the new in life. America has a modern mind.'

The University Library, in the same striped architecture, stood beside the Henry Ford Building, hiding from general view the Otto Suhr Institute for Political Research and the Institute for Research into East European Studies. The Science faculties, so Götz explained, were scattered in the green suburbs of West Berlin. For the more technically minded there was another entire university, the *Technische Hochschule* in the heart of the city near the Bismarck Allee, a dull, conventional university compared with the FU.

'This university is perhaps the most unique in Germany,' Götz told me as he sipped his coffee. The terrace was crowded with intense, bearded students, with pretty girls in knee length skirts and lambs' wool sweaters, wearing pearls and lockets that dangled round their necks. 'I have lived in Berlin all my life and I know what the FU means to the city. It is a symbol of the new Germany.'

The old university of Berlin was in the Russian sector. After the war it was re-named the Humboldt and became nothing more than the instrument of communist propaganda. The American General, Lucius Clay, gave permission to the West Berliners to build a Free University in the American Sector. In 1948 the Free University was founded as the first autonomous university of Germany. The Rector was chosen by the Mayor of West Berlin and given complete authority and independence. He supervised the finances of the University in conjunction with an advisory body. *Asta* was granted special privileges and a broader curriculum was introduced along American and British lines. From the start the University had an extensive degree of independence that merited the name, 'Free University'.

Of the fifteen thousand students enrolled at the FU almost half came from West Germany. The most popular subjects were philosophy, economic and social science, and medicine. However, it was the Institute of Political Science that really dominated the University, attracting as it did, some of the most stimulating professors and a large number of left-wing students: It greatly increased the interest in politics and maintained a strong left-wing trend. Several members of *Asta* studied at the Institute.

Not only was the FU *Asta* more political than its counterpart at Freiburg, but it also had a greater share in the administration of the University. That students should play an active part in the running of the FU was part of its conception. The *Asta* largely controlled the *Klausur*, a system of selection by which almost twenty per cent of applicants to the FU were refused admission. In the early days of the University, the first *Asta* had abolished the student clubs, the *Burschenschaften*. It was felt that these clubs propagated an *élite*, based not on merit but on snobbery, and were responsible for much faction through the jealousy they aroused.

I attended a general meeting of the Student Union in the Henry Ford Building. Representatives of the different faculties discussed questions of social welfare, student housing, grants and examinations, with the members of *Asta*. In the back row of the dimly lit hall I spoke to one of the twelve members of *Asta*. She was a third year student of political science, clever and blunt. 'We were elected as much for our political beliefs as for our capacity to deal with the administration of a university. We have never hidden the fact that most of us belong to the SDS (the German Socialist Student Union). To protest against American intervention in Vietnam is as important to us as social welfare of the students.'

In the most recent battle with the Rector (the battle that had aroused so much enthusiasm in Freiburg) *Asta* had taken a stand on its right to mix politics with the university administration. 'The University gave us a vote of confidence,' the girl told me proudly. 'It is no use people complaining that we are too political. That is how we see our role.' The administrative reforms that *Asta* proposed were undefined and nebulous. The enemy was not the Rector but the professors in general. They were accused of being old-fashioned and unwilling to contemplate any change in the curriculum.

On reform of the examination system *Asta* had more precise ideas. 'Assistant professors should be invested with more powers,' said one member. 'They understand that the present system of examinations is ludicrously unfair. We ask to be given marks throughout the year, so that our whole future is not decided in a few hours.' On this point *Asta* had the sympathy of most students at the University. Götz felt that the present examinations placed inhuman pressure on candidates. 'I have several friends who crack up completely before their examinations. Others defer the terrible date from year to year and sometimes cannot bring themselves to sit their Finals at all.' He recognised that the system was undergoing a change : new proposals had been accepted to shorten courses and reorganise examinations so that several minor examinations would replace the all important major Final that came at the end of six or seven years' study. However, Götz saw little hope of improving university conditions. Despite the *Klausur*, the FU was already overcrowded. 'We don't see much of our professors, or even of our assistant professors,' Götz told me. Seminars in the most popular courses were more like lectures with too many students to allow for any individual interchange of thought.

In the Institute of Political Thought where the intake was strictly controlled this was not the case. I sat in on several lectures and seminars; the atmosphere was informal and personal. I had a long and interesting discussion with a charming lecturer, Herr Winkler, a man in his early thirties who was about to leave for America on a Harvard Research Scholarship. He taught Modern History. Interest in the Weimar Republic was universal, he told me. 'My students have passionate feelings. It is almost impossible for them to understand the rise of the Nazi Party. However, I, as an historian, must account for it, though not, of course, excuse it.'

I was impressed by his manner of teaching. He did not lecture but talked to his students. He felt that a new attitude to teaching was necessary. 'A professor can maintain his old status of demi-god at one of the traditional universities, Heidelberg or Freiburg, but in the FU he has to modify his attitude. This is a violent university. The young are industrious, often stimulating, and unusually arrogant. They have no respect for their parents' generation, which is indeed understandable, and they are very impatient.'

At the FU, more than at any university I had ever visited, I found a passionate and universal interest in the social and political problems of the new Germany. In England I discovered a counterpart in Sussex University where I sensed the same degree of involvement when I spent a week-end there a year later. American influence revealed itself in both universities in the curricula and in the emphasis on sociology and studies of the mind and of human behaviour.

At the Henry Ford Building I read posters in lurid colours announcing discussions on sex, psychology and sex, neurology and sex, Christianity and sex, and urbanology. Yet it was modern politics that aroused the most intense interest. Political attitudes were often undefined and fierce because they had not yet established a framework in which they could develop. The war had deprived Germany of its right to be nationalist. The post-war wave of anti-nationalism led to the development of an international concept of politics. Among students it had assumed two forms. One was an international socialism that was to create either a federal socialist state with the East European Countries, or a violently revolutionary country that would inflame the world with its ideal democracy. The second was a federal democratic state of Europe in which the present institutions and liberties of European countries would survive. Both concepts involved the major powers. Either Germany was to draw closer to Western Europe, which meant closer relations with America, or was to withdraw from the web of capitalism to create closer ties with the East. Marxist doctrine directed many students into the eastern camp; in *Asta*, where politics were pursued with missionary zeal, it had found ardent supporters.

The *Asta* offices were in a small English, suburban-type house on a street that ran parallel to the university campus. I passed through small, crowded rooms. Walls were thick with posters and tables staggered under the weight of copies of the *Asta*

newspaper, the *FU Spiegel*. The head of the Department of
Political Information was sorting posters giving the dates and
times of a film showing the sufferings of the North Vietnamese.
In a chaotic office I met the President, Herr Harmuth. He had
small but bright eyes, a round face and an oddly pointed chin.
He explained that the disputes between *Asta* and the Rector
arose from their conflicting conceptions of the University. 'He
wants to keep politics out of the University, whereas we want
to greatly increase its role.' It was one of *Asta*'s major proposals that a course in political theory should become obligatory, as it was at the Humboldt University. Not only the left
point of view would be put forward (in this assertion I had
little faith): 'Everyone would be free to form their own political
opinions, but a knowledge of the problems that face society is
essential to students if they are to contribute to modern life,'
Herr Harmuth stated nobly. He felt that the ordinary people
should also receive a political education, and that only thus
would they become more involved in the running of the country
and take a greater interest in its administration. He envisaged the
development of a socialist state without violence, through a more
extensive political education in and out of the universities.

Herr Harmuth disliked the Bonn Government intensely. As
a Socialist he had been bitterly disappointed in his Party for
accepting membership of the grand coalition with the Christian
Democrats. He felt that it was not a natural alliance but a be-
trayal of the socialist movement. 'The SPD has compromised
itself,' he said. 'There is no left-wing party in Germany any
more, no effective opposition to the Government. The political
situation is unevenly balanced and dangerous and will inevitably
encourage extremism.'

The extreme left-wing students of the FU had formed into
small groups and lived a communal life in 'digs' in West Berlin.
I asked Herr Harmuth what he thought of the students from
the *Kommune*, who had attempted to throw a pudding at Vice-
President Humphrey on his visit to Berlin. Five had, as a result,
been suspended from the university. 'We dissociated ourselves
from these students as soon as we heard of the incident. They
are not part of our movement.' He added, 'However, in the past
our views have coincided. We have marched together against
American imperialism and intervention in Vietnam, and we will

no doubt join together in the coming protest march against the
visit of the Shah of Persia.' (It was this visit that set the revolutionary student movement in Germany in motion.) In the past
the *Asta* newspaper had printed articles from the revolutionaries.
I had read one that advocated in corny catch phrases the destruc-
tion of the Establishment and the reconstruction of a truly
democratic society. Herr Harmuth felt that the revolutionaries
were wasting their energies in abstract political philosophy.
'Many among them are not students, but vagabond agitators.'
With a tinge of sarcasm he added, 'Their main topic of discussion is their own sex problems and free love.'

He was wrong. The street stood near the railway station in
the notorious crime district of Berlin. Litter and dirt filled the
gutter. On the fifth floor of a block of flats I rang a door bell.
A girl in jeans and a long, white sweater opened the door and
stood with a patient, quizzical expression. 'Are you the *Kommune*?' I asked. She hesitated, then said, 'Yes, I suppose that's
us,' and showed me into the 'press room' where five young
men were sorting leaflets and articles that lay in stacks on long
wooden tables. They looked at me, an evident *bourgeoise*, with
unconcealed suspicion.

I swallowed hard when I saw these five farouche faces. One
boy had bright red hair that swamped his face and ended in
a long red beard. Another peered through horn-rimmed glasses
from a mass of black curls which fell to his shoulders. A tall,
feline young man wore giant red flowered earrings. His colleague, whose rugged dark brown skin reminded me of a gypsy,
asked from behind a pile of paper what exactly I had come
for. I muttered an embarrassed explanation. The Heathcliff of
the group showed me into an adjoining room. A double bed
propped up in a corner was unmade; blankets and pillows
covered the four mattresses set at different corners of the room;
broken chairs stood round a low table and thick dust on the
windows obliterated the back view of the station. We sat around
the table. I answered sharp questions fired by the swarthy German. After a few minutes he seemed satisfied that I was not a
spy and began to talk about the aim of the *Kommune*.

'We are setting an example for others to follow,' he began.
Dirt clung to his face. The room smelled, and dust lay thick on
the wooden floor boards. Looking round the squalid, sordid

room I said to myself, 'you must be joking,' though I knew he wasn't. 'Everything must be changed,' he went on. 'Society is rotten. The rich exploit the poor. Only a revolution can free men from their oppressors.' He paused. 'We believe in Communism, so we lead a communal life and share everything, and discuss our problems freely.'

I asked on whose money the *Kommune* lived. 'Together we find enough to pay the rent and to buy food. One of us held a scholarship before he was suspended from the University. The girls are still supported by their parents,' said the swarthy German. I asked tentatively if it was not a denial of their doctrine to live off the *bourgeoisie*. 'It is the best we can do for the moment,' he answered sharply. As an afterthought he added, 'We got some money from the Humphrey scandal. People had to pay to interview us.'

The young man in earrings and his friend with the red beard came in to listen to the conversation. Red beard was not a student, but to those who were, revolutionary work was far more important that the university. I learned that they were in contact with the anarchists in Amsterdam, with Chinese students, with French anarchists, with Belgian Communists. 'There is constant communication between us,' said the young man. 'At the moment people laugh at us, but as you can see we are quite serious. Our time will come.' I asked about East German communism. 'Rubbish,' red beard burst out, 'nothing but rubbish. Even Russia shows signs of betraying the cause.' Who then did they follow I asked. Certainly not the Russian regime. Much of Mao Tse-tung's philosophy they admired – the cultural revolution and the Red Guard were perhaps the strongest influence. Che Guevara was the most undisputed hero and Castro had effectuated the most recent worthwhile revolution. 'Every revolution has its own character,' said the young man in earrings. 'The Marxist state has never been successfully established, not because it is impossible but because men are too weak and selfish. If enough people are prepared to take up arms and fight the Establishment, just as we here have set up by ourselves, it could not fail.'

This young man in earrings, the most perspicacious of the group, asked quite suddenly if I would ever join a *Kommune*. I shook my head and said quite frankly that I did not want to leave my family. Astonishment burned on all faces. I realised that they had not considered that I was an open enemy. They bristled like cats and attacked with questions: 'What does your father do?' 'Where were you educated? Your brother goes to Oxford? Oh, my God!' 'What are you going to do about the rotten society?'

When I commented that I wanted to be a writer and that I thought books had great influence over men they threw back their heads with hysterical laughter. The mood changed to anger when I ventured to say that if Marx had not written *Das Kapital* they would have little to say for themselves. Red beard growled in despair when I said that it was not the time for revolution but for peaceful changes within the structure of democracy without murder or war. 'Come back to us when you can smell the stench of the world,' he snarled. I asked who had written the article in the *FU Spiegel*. A voice behind the black curls muttered, 'I did.' Meekly and perhaps superfluously, though the thought was honest, I said it was well written. Red beard expostulated and cried, glaring at his friends, 'My God, you must be a lousy writer if she thinks it was good. She's a bloody *Spiessbürgerin.*'

The door opened and two girls walked in. One, a thin girl with long black hair, walked up to the boy with red earrings and sat on his knee. She looked at me and asked doubtfully, 'Is she interested in joining?' The boy laughed. 'She's a lost cause.' Red beard burst in again and sat on one of the mattresses. 'I don't know what you are talking politics for. You'll never get through to her. She might be good to sleep with but that's about all. Tell us about your sexual problems,' he said suddenly and burst out laughing. Perhaps the President of *Asta* was right after all. I shook hands with everyone as I left. I was shown out by the boy with earrings; the others sat with their feet on the low table and their laughter followed me to the door.

I shall never forget this meeting. It opened my eyes to a new student movement that was, during the following years, to reach the headlines of the world Press. I discovered a determination to revolt and to destroy that I had only read about and never seen for myself. On the subject of revolution my ideas were to undergo many changes but they were stimulated by my stay in West Berlin.

To the majority of students at the FU the revolutionaries were dismissed as extremists who would have no influence over the university as a whole. Götz saw no future in their communal life. 'The fear of communism in West Germany eliminates the possibility of any extensive swing to the left,' he felt. With great seriousness he added, 'They are dangerous only because they cause a reaction to the right.'

As Vice-President of the Young European movement, Götz spent little time at the University and saw it only in terms of lectures and seminars. West Berlin was a major centre of the movement that thrived under the auspices of the *Europazentrum*. Every year Götz helped organise student congresses that were attended by delegates from all over Europe, including England. He found the French Young Europeans the most stimulating, though a little pedantic in their observance of etiquette. 'They address each other formally,' he told me with a smile, 'and have elaborate titles, vice-presidents, sub-vice-presidents, vice-sub-vice-presidents, which we are expected to remember in all seating arrangements.'

The Young Europeans were, like their socialist counterparts, concerned with the question, '*Wozu?*' (What for?) In what ideological direction were the enormous energies of young Germans to be channelled? Germany was in a state of material prosperity, but where was the outlet for the moral passions of its youth? *Asta* members sought a socialist state, while conservatives still dreamed of a unified Germany. Götz and his friends felt convinced that Germany could only re-emerge in a new federal Europe. 'She is a country without an identity,' Götz exclaimed. 'In a federal Europe she could regain her identity and would not arouse in other countries the fear that she was reviving nationalism for military ends.' He was afraid, however, that Europe might not develop fast enough and that Germany would be seriously threatened by the right-wing neo-Nazi Party, the NPD.

In the strong left-wing atmosphere of the FU I was surprised to find even one member of the NPD. *Asta* informed me that a year before a student of twenty-six, a member of the NPD, had stood as a candidate in the elections of the *Studentenrat*, and had suffered a crushing defeat. I located him after two weeks of extensive enquiries and he invited me to visit him in his flat.

He was a tall, thin man, with a light brown moustache. Unusually large pupils eclipsed the blue of his eyes. He wore a dark suit with a tie and spoke slowly in a hard Berlin accent. In the neat flat a gramophone played a recording of German marching songs of the last war. During much of our conversation he gave me the official NPD line.

'Our judgement of history is more objective than that of many countries. Hitler rose to power because of the unfair treatment that Germany received from the hands of England and America at the end of the First World War. As for the outbreak of the Second World War, we do not eliminate the possibility that England urged Poland to oppose and even invade Germany. With English help the Poles planned to occupy Germany up to the Oder, to take Berlin and set up a federation of Eastern Europe with Czecho-Slovakia. Hitler was largely provoked into war.'

On the subject of the mass murder of the Jews I felt sick to my stomach. Placidly the young man explained that, though distorted history claims to the contrary, persecution of the Jews began in 1939 and not before. 'England bombed our towns and killed our civilians long before we bombed her cities. German hatred reached its highest pitch and the Germans took their revenge on the Jews. It was a natural reaction.' He admitted, with a shrug, that mass murder was a crime. 'Not only the Germans were to blame. Many of the guards at the concentration camps were foreigners.'

Germany would be great again. All foreign workers should return to their own countries and politicians should concentrate on re-establishing lost nationalism. Europe might unite but no federation would ever be possible since Germany could not sacrifice her national pride.

I could listen no more. As I left I asked what percentage of West Germans were followers of the NPD. 'Of young people under thirty-five say fifty per cent,' he told me emphatically. I asked why then did he not get one single vote when he proposed himself as a candidate for *Asta*. He shuffled his feet. 'They were all Marxists. They did not represent the university.' Though the opinions of *Asta* were considered too extreme by the majority of students on the subject of the NPD, Europeans, revolutionaries and conservatives were united. The neo-Nazi Party was the common enemy.

Politics were not every student's first love. I met Ferdinand, a fat, jovial young European at the book stand of the West Berlin station. He was buying a copy of '*Mad*' magazine. It was a sunny afternoon and he invited me to tea in his room in the residential campus, the Student Village.

It lay near the Wannsee. Twenty-three low buildings in heavy brick and a *Mensa* stood gloomily in a compound separated from each other by sick trees and thin brown grass. Ferdinand conducted me to his room. In the entrance hall we stepped over coloured paper and empty boxes. 'Last night we had a party. Two hundred people.' I found a notice advertising hot dogs at one mark. 'Next week Number Twelve Building is giving a party. They plan to install a bath on the lawn and put up advertisements for " Midnight Bathing ".' His room was small and gay, plastered with pictures of film stars, looking on to the grass and bushes. The sun was unusually hot for May and bodies holding books or lying prostrate in bathing suits dotted the lawn. I noticed a classic scene worthy of Manet. Under a tree at the edge of the lawn a serious man with a pointed nose, red hair and spectacles, sat bolt upright in a wooden chair typing furiously on the table in front of him.

Ferdinand introduced me to a group of his friends, a Turk, a north Italian and two Germans. The Italian was looking at a distant group of girls in bikinis. The Turk lay in a deck chair holding his stomach. 'I've got ulcers,' he explained, 'but my doctor doesn't seem to care.' On the walls of his room the Turk had pinned giant photographs from *Playboy*. The Italian, from the cold north, kept a supply of energy pills by his desk. While listening to records in the Italian's room, which also looked on to the lawn, we watched the Turk make a clumsy pass at a German friend of his. 'It's not good for your ulcers,' she said positively and left to make cold tea.

Any student could apply for a room at the *Studentendorf* where food and lodging were cheap. Life at the Student Village was organised by a specially elected parliament that made laws, arbitrated and took most administrative decisions. The films or discussions with guest speakers from the university, the parties and debates held in the student bar, that took place almost every night created a university life far more intimate than in the FU. A student film club presented a weekly film about life in the community. Throughout the week a 'hidden' camera had peered from bushes and roof tops, to capture immortal scenes for the weekly showing. A sarcastic commentary complemented the entertaining and sometimes embarrassing film, which inevitably attracted a good humoured audience.

The sky clouded over. Figures climbed through windows into their rooms and re-emerged in trousers and sweaters. A fat, middle-aged man came up to our group. 'You made too much noise at your party last night,' he announced sourly. 'Someone has complained to the student parliament.' There was a general outcry. The Italian boy asked what bastard had lodged the complaint. 'Some Sicilian in House Twelve,' said the dour faced man. 'A Sicilian!' cried the Milanese. 'I might have guessed. I know the one. A nasty little boy from the south. All day long he sits around doing nothing and when we have a party he complains. *Mamma mia*! How insensitive.' We sat and drank cold tea and watched the last sunbathers drag themselves into their rooms to change into warmer clothes. Only the thin man, still typing intensely, did not look up from his work.

Ferdinand decided that the day should not end with the sun. 'We must go on a *Bummel*,' he announced. I learned that a *Bummel* was a whistle stop tour of beer cellars and night clubs. Giuliano, the Italian, offered to make up the party with his Swedish girl-friend, a pretty, vacant blonde who sat on the lawn reading an American comic.

Ferdinand's Volkswagen splurted, jerked and, to our relief, stopped. We had arrived at the Leidecke-*Kneipe* (the German word for bar), a remnant of 'old' Berlin. Its dirty wooden floor and student posters pinned to the walls reminded me of Saint Germain. From behind a screen of cigarette smoke a loud shout 'Ferdinand' greeted us and then through the thick air a young man emerged and invited us to join his table. I sat next to a friend of his, a man of twenty-three who looked more like a child of ten. His skin was white and his red cheeks seemed absurdly like apples. He paid no attention to the rest of the table but sat kissing his girl-friend passionately. Ferdinand whispered to me that the boy was a great friend of his, 'With complicated sex problems,' he added darkly. Not surprising, I thought, when I saw the food he had ordered. In front of the preoccupied young man the waitress placed a plate of raw minced meat, topped with a raw egg, surrounded by oysters.

Feeling merry and full of wine, we left the cellar at midnight. 'Now for some exercise,' Ferdinand announced. From a quiet street that echoed with the gentle sound of rain, we pushed our way through a narrow door into a blast of music, laughter, bright lights and choking cigarette smoke. The Old Eden was the most popular night club of West Berlin, mainly because it charged no entrance fee. Drinks were cheap and diversion endless. In the entrance room students gathered around the bar. Giant umbrellas and frightening skeletons hung from the ceiling which was covered with slogans and paintings. Posters, effigies and mascots cluttered the walls. Three projector screens attracted a large audience; one flashed dull advertisements; another nude photographs; a third was projecting four films at the same time, which ran conjointly dividing the screen into four small squares. We had the choice between Charlie Chaplin and Brigitte Bardot, *Sunset at Dead Man's Creek* and *I Was A Teenage Werewolf*. The stools and tables were all taken. People, mainly students, packed the bar which faced the three screens. Giuliano and his girl-friend miraculously found a seat, where we left them shrouded in cigarette smoke, the girl drinking and Giuliano casting surreptitious glances at the naked ladies.

I followed Ferdinand up the vertical iron ladder to an elevated platform six feet above the ground. We sat eye-level to the screens. Before I became totally engrossed in *I Was A Teenage Werewolf*, I noticed a sputnik go by. I blinked and looked again. Attached to a rail a tin sputnik travelled from the far side of the room to the bar. When it arrived at the bar, the barmaid opened the side of the sputnik, took out three empty glasses, filled them with beer, and sent them back again. A thirsty customer had only to ring the ship's bell that hung from the ceiling and his empty glass would be carried away by the obliging, ingenious spacecraft.

Ferdinand did not share my passion for *I Was A Teenage Werewolf*, so we struggled through the crowd into the night club, where it wasn't possible to move without hitting one of the hot bodies that crammed the floor. The Germans did not seem entertaining nor rhythmical dancers, but I admired their patience and persistence : they reiterated the same step hour upon hour. Sweaty and bedraggled we staggered through the fumes of the hamburger stand, past a small room where a negro band was singing soul music into the wet cool air of the night. Ferdinand decided that we needed a complete contrast. 'To the Fat Chicken,' he shouted.

The entrance to The Fat Chicken was a door built into a giant wine barrel ten feet high. Inside, the deep red rooms were set at different angles to each other; on the walls hung modern paintings in subdued colours. The chairs and tables might have belonged to a boudoir. We drank wine and spoke in a whisper. Our *Bummel* had fizzled out.

There was an anarchical sense of freedom in West Berlin even on the rainiest of days. While the FU rotated in a ceaseless fermentation of ideas, the same attitude of experiment and discovery showed itself in the modern architecture of the city. In the park near the Brandenburg Gate I stood fascinated by the original and extraordinary conceptions of the Congress Hall, the Academy of Art, with an experimental stage that could be viewed simultaneously by two separate audiences. More than any other building, the Philharmonic – a totally asymmetric and intriguing construction, presenting a different outline at every angle – released a sense of energy and unfettered expansion. I felt the same freedom of expression when I visited the *Kunst Hochschule* where both Bettina and Ulrich had studied and indeed first met. Ulrich had been a sculptor at the time. 'He was appallingly rude about my drawings,' Bettina recalled indignantly. 'I thought he was a thug.' One of the most famous teachers at the Art School was a Mr Gonda. I had met him one evening and was delighted when he invited me to his studio.

The *Meister*, with the positive step of one who knows his own importance, walked into the *Kunst Hochschule* on the Hardenberg Strasse. I trotted behind the famous Polish artist, along white-washed corridors used by students as a storage room for their finished works, past stone pillars, open courtyards, brick walls coated in ivy, past a small garden stifled by an excess of trees. 'A nunnery or a lunatic asylum,' Gonda muttered as he pushed open the door of his studio.

Gonda, like all other teachers at the *Hochschule,* had been invited to set up a studio in the Art School on the basis of his work as an artist. In his studio he had the right to carry out his own work undisturbed. In his charge were ten to fifteen students chosen by him from a short list. The eight hundred students at the *Hochschule,* the biggest in West Germany, represented a quarter of the students who had applied to the School.

'I doubt if you'll see many students today,' Mr Gonda said. 'It is Saturday and I dare say they are sailing or swimming.' He explained that as a teacher he did not interfere with the work of his students. They had complete freedom to experiment in any form of artistic expression. 'I can advise and criticise, but I never dictate. They come and go as they please,' and as he opened the door to a larger classroom, he added, 'and today it looks as if they have gone.'

The large room was empty except for a bearded artist who stood in front of a huge, undefined form in papier mâché. Extraordinary plastic, iron and even paper forms stood in different corners of the room. The young man with the thick black beard was working at what looked like a wire tree; teacups dangled and clattered from its branches. I thought I had seen him at the station with a group of hippies standing under the time-table. The *Bahnhof,* with its dirt and confusion, had more character than any other single building in West Berlin. The art student had a kind, distant expression and hardly looked up from his work. As we went out Gonda told me that he was an excellent student, 'Only he is never off pot.' He went on, 'They tell me that it gives them greater inner perception. I am quite willing to believe this, although as yet I am in need of proof.'

Mr Gonda told me that through the Berlin Wall the Art School had lost the source of its best talent. 'Students in the East have to battle to get to the *Kunst Hochschule.* Those who came to us were exceptionally good, more talented than students in the West.' The top grade students were granted permission to stay on at the Art School for a fifth year and were given an entire studio to themselves. Mr Gonda liked his students to use all kinds of materials. Plastics, rubber, wire, even papier mâché. 'I have no wish for them to copy my own style,' he said.

In his studio several of his works were on display. Mr Gonda was a sculptor and worked mainly in bronze and stone. I stared at the shapes and forms that resembled nothing, yet riveted the eye. Mr Gonda tried to explain the change in art that had taken place since the Second World War. As children he and his friends had sat in the courtyards of the *Kunst Hochschule* and drawn portraits of each other or of trees. 'Today not one of my students is interested in reproducing either his fellow human beings or nature. Science has invaded the modern world.' He claimed that in the present age men thought for the masses. The individual man was no longer the centre of the universe. 'An artist must find a new way in which to express this cosmic feeling.' Through art he could contribute to modern thought; he could create shapes of the future and stimulate new thoughts. The artist no longer had a duty to reproduce. 'He seeks a less individual form of expression for a less individual world.'

I do not doubt that to any connoisseur of modern art these words appear trite. To me they were a minor revelation. I understood for the first time that the comment, 'but it doesn't look like anything,' was irrelevant. 'You must teach your eyes to see,' the sculptress under whom I had studied in Rome, had once told me. I felt, during the morning I spent at the Art School, that Mr Gonda was offering a key to the 'language' of modern art.

At times I felt that the 'key' to modern Germany lay in the FU. It mirrored every shade of political opinion, it was a battleground for the ideas and problems that face my generation. Surrounded by East Germany the atmosphere was inevitably tense. If you went out, you danced till dawn; if you marched, you threw a bomb; if you studied, you worked all night; if you were an artist, you welded iron. The presence of East Berlin, the distance from West Germany, the acute awareness of living in a young democracy were added inducements to extreme opinions and potential violence.

One of the most intelligent German students I met, Eghart

Essler, a student at Heidelberg, felt that the FU, in an exaggerated form, reflected all the problems of conscience that faced his generation. 'It is difficult to be young in West Germany,' he told me. 'You cannot glorify anything in the past. In the war we had no heroes, only villains.' He felt in the new democracy the absence of any secure structure. 'Our country is in embryo; materially it is advanced, but politically and morally it vacillates between extremes.'

In 1948 the German statesman Friedrich Meinecke, a sick man at the time, said on the foundation of the new Free University, '*Mit Freude höre ich die Stimme der Jugend, begrüsse ich ihre Forderung nach einer neuen Universität, nach einer wirklichen Freistätte der Wissenschaft und deren Lehre.*' But does freedom to study what you wish produce freedom of thought? Does the absence of intellectual discipline produce tolerance? I preferred German to French universities, yet I remained plagued with doubt.

7

Oxford

June 1967

IT was a fast trip across East Germany to Brunswick, where I collected my duffle bag, then on through northern Germany to Leiden. On the way I spent a few hours at the new University of Bochum; the enormous grey skyscrapers merged against a background of oil refineries and gas storage tanks. Smog and drizzle, damp sticky air, scaffolding of unfinished faculties, dull faces: I couldn't stand the morbidly depressing atmosphere. I left coughing and spluttering and drove as fast as I could to Holland.

I stayed three days in Leiden but hardly saw the daylight. My cousin, Wick Holtz, a brilliant and eccentric Dutchman, was in his last year of law at the University. He took me to two all-night parties where I met his friends; they spoke impeccable English, were alarmingly intelligent and often witty. Since we slept for most of the day I saw little of the town. However, on the third day I sacrificed sleep to catch a glimpse of Leiden, of its river and narrow bridges, of its beautiful churches and eighteenth century buildings, of its winding streets alive with students on bicycles.

My short stay was over all too soon. I drove through the night to Calais, then sat on the deck of the Channel steamer in the wet grey mist and thought of June in England, of Oxford, where my brother was finishing his first year of history at Magdalen College. The fog lifted to reveal a bright warm sun and I was sitting on lawns that spread out to all four sides of the Magdalen cloisters. Of the colleges at Oxford, Christ Church and Magdalen are to me the most beautiful. Christ Church is more impressive and majestic, Magdalen the gentler.

It has been filmed, painted and described and I shall only add a short paragraph to the reams already printed.

It is old, sixteenth century, and sings of Elizabeth and Ye Olde England. Go through the porter's lodge and into the forecourt of the college and you stand on green grass and face the President's house, low and quaint. Ivy clings to the walls of the older buildings, gargoyles and stone carvings frame the Tudor windows. The stained-glass windows of the Chapel are lifeless from the outside, but inside they glint and paint the hall with gentle colours. The buildings of St Swithin's lead on to more neatly kept lawns and to the park. Deer graze in the tall grass in front of heavy trees. A croquet lawn stretches in front of the New Building, a perfectly rectangular, long, off-white structure, with paint decorously peeling from its walls. Andrew looked around him with great pleasure. ' If you don't get anything else out of Oxford, you learn to appreciate beauty,' he said. Rather a charming remark, I thought, for a brother.

This I had realised in the course of the morning when we visited Merton, the inner quad at All Souls, the Christchurch Meadows, and the Bodleian Library before it was time for lunch at Magdalen.

Inmates of the all male college, some with bare chests, sunbathed on the grass. A few sporadic girls chewed chicken bones or sat looking picturesque in hats. My brother had gone to fetch lager from the college bar. Clive Gibson, his face framed in blond curls, looked, from upside down, like the original potto; he was talking about the Magdalen play *Midsummer Night's Dream* that he had helped produce in the park, amid the deer and the trees. ' They are all so lucky,' I thought as I watched a cloud get caught on the four spires of Magdalen tower. They didn't face any of the problems that preoccupied students throughout Europe. The University cannot be overcrowded because it is residential. A girl or boy applies to one of the twenty-three male, or five female, colleges for a place to read a certain subject. If they are accepted they come into residence and live at the University for the three eight-week terms in the year. For the first two years a girl has her own room in the college, and for her third year she moves out into digs in the town. A man has his own room in his first year and, in his second, he has a sitting-room as well. For the two years he lives in college he is looked after by a 'scout' who cleans his room, delivers messages and sees his clothes are washed.

Each college is autonomous, with a President and a Dean. Though the proctors administer the general university law, each college devises its own rules, and the Dean acts as judge. Oxford has been aptly described as a federation of colleges.

A college does not confine its intake to students in one particular subject, but accepts an equal number of students in all subjects. 'Not only do you meet and live among people from every type of background, but you also get to know people who study subjects totally different from your own,' Andrew told me. He felt that the collegiate system is one of Oxford's greatest advantages. Though it doesn't prevent the initial feeling of loneliness, eventually it gives undergraduates the chance to meet and make friends with a wide cross section of students, and gives the University a more closely knit atmosphere.

At Oxford the majority of undergraduates come from grammar schools, the equivalent of an American high school, run on a competitive basis. The grants system in England, regulated according to parental income, provides a living 'wage' for all students during the term time. The grants cover university fees and an adequate standard of maintenance. 'No man in England can claim that he is too poor to send his children to university,' said Lord James, the Vice Chancellor of York University. This is true. Though the public schools with their more individual teaching methods give children a better chance of getting to the best universities, it is significant that in English universities the proportion of students from working class families is the highest in Europe.

Two American tourists appeared on the lawn. 'Isn't it just too perfect, Henry,' said a plump lady in plimsolls, as she and Henry gazed on the delicate stone arches of the cloisters. 'If only we could take it home with us . . .' she sighed. 'They'll have London Bridge next,' Clive muttered with remarkable foresight.

Beside the Americans stood a startling blonde in a brown leather mini-dress; she wandered on to the grass looking self-consciously lost.

'Not a bad bit of fluff,' Michael Hart informed his friends. 'Wouldn't mind showing her around. I'm an excellent tourist guide.'

'Far too pretty to be an undergraduate. She's imported,' Andrew announced, 'A foreigner at a secretarial college.' There are several in Oxford, as well as finishing schools and St. Clare's, a branch of London University, not famed for academics.

'Probably wants to sample undergraduate life like all these foreigners that pour into Oxford. I could give her an idea,' Michael went on ... but it was too late. She glanced vacantly at the staring faces and left.

'There are seven men to every girl at this university. Twenty-three men's colleges and five women's, and most Oxford girls are very ugly,' he pouted, 'and those who aren't are pursued by every man in Oxford. It's a tough life,' he concluded.

'You bring it on yourself,' a friend of his retorted. 'Girls aren't worth the trouble. Too much strain. Unless you are prepared to take them out night after night they lose interest. Most of them are so ludicrously moral. You have to be the big thing in their lives or you're cut from the picture.'

'Oxford isn't geared for girls,' Andrew chimed in. 'Where do you take them. No good night clubs. It's either a cup of coffee, a snack in a Wimpy or the cinema.'

'Not much chance for free love at Oxford with the rules we've got,' a bare chested youth moaned. Though Oxford is prepared for anything, with six birth control centres, I learnt that girls had to be out of the rooms by midnight, and undergraduates were supposed to be in their rooms by one. But Andrew had shown me the dip in the Magdalen wall where for several hundred years students had climbed into the college at all times of the night, after the gates were shut. He pointed out a ladder that had been at the other side of the wall. 'The college was sick of having to repair its bicycle shed,' he told me, 'so they decided to put up a ladder so that anyone climbing over would no longer have to jump on the tin roof.' Very broad-minded, I thought.

Robin Lane Fox, a brilliant classics scholar and an old friend, arrived. His rooms were in the cloisters, as he pointed out to me. He looked sunburnt, tall with blond hair and very healthy. 'I've just handed in an essay on Greek botany. My tutor said it was a remarkable piece of undergraduate work, and it was.' Robin scowled when he saw a nearby group of bare-chested undergraduates lying prostrate in the sun. 'It's so unaesthetic,' he grumbled, 'and why should we have their hairy tits in our lunch?'

Robin worked extremely hard. He had already got a first in the first half of his degree. (Each degree is marked in three categories, first, second and third. The second is divided into an upper and a lower second, a two one and a two two.)

At Oxford lectures are not compulsory and undergraduates are taught by tutors. Just as students are affiliated to a college, so are most of the academic staff of the University, either as dons or fellows. Generally a student is taught by a don, or a fellow or a professor of his college, though often he may go to a don in another college if his subject is unusual.

Andrew described his tutorials to me. He had one a week, but would soon have more. For each tutorial he had to prepare an essay on some enormous subject such as the maritime policy in the reign of Elizabeth I. 'You are given a huge reading list that you can't possibly complete and you sit up the night before writing furiously.' His tutorial was held in his tutor's house. 'My tutorial is at ten, and often when I arrive, the man is hardly out of bed. " Have a drink, have a drink," he mutters as he goes off to shave.'

'You can say anything you like to your tutor,' Robin said, 'and he might say anything to you.' At the beginning of the summer term he had gone to a new tutor for Greek philosophy. As he had walked into the room he was greeted with the remark 'I hope you are not a queer, Fox, I can't stand queers.' Robin assured him that he was not and, from then on, they got on very well. 'A tutor is more a critic than a teacher. You work by yourself, read in the holidays, write essays in the term. He doesn't set a pace, you do. And if you haven't done enough work by the exams you get a bad degree.'

The whole emphasis of the tutorials is on thinking for yourself. Michael recalled one essay he had written at the last minute. 'My tutor had, as is often the case in Oxford, written a book on the subject. I bought his book and reproduced his ideas. He was furious. "I didn't set you an essay just to regurgitate what I have written. You are here to think for yourself," he growled.'

Lunch was over. Andrew and I walked through the narrow streets of Oxford, past small, brightly coloured houses, squashed together in uneven lines. I could see into green gardens, half hidden behind college fronts built in beautiful yellow stone. We walked along the famous Broad Street and the High, pushed our way along the pavements crowded with students and shoppers. The streets were jammed with cars and students on bicycles. As we walked farther away from the centre I noticed the spires and towers that rose above the noisy town. We rang the bell of a dull, red-brick house.

Paul Butler, in his last year of history, thin, with curly hair and a shrewd face, was re-heating the breakfast that his landlady had brought him while he was still asleep. He had digs on the road leading out of Oxford towards Banbury. Three years ago he had won an open history scholarship to Christ Church.

'People look busy,' he yawned, 'because they are busy,' and he stared at his smoking toast. 'Most people take part in some university project. The clubs and societies cover every kind of interest. If you collect grasshoppers you'll find a club to join. Otherwise you just start your own.' A friend of his had, the week before, started an Apathetic Society. 'I am an honorary member. We inaugurated the club with a bottle of sherry in this room. We did nothing. It was a huge success.'

Paul described the historical clubs, the law, classics, philosophy, political and arts societies, the music, drama, painting and sculpture clubs, and the athletic societies. He explained that dons and professors were willing to preside over the more erudite societies, and lead the intellectual ' work-outs ' (the highbrow meetings) that take place behind the thick walls of Balliol. 'The academic staff lives in Oxford, we see our tutors constantly. They take an interest in undergraduate ideas, they don't segregate themselves, and at times you have an intellectual life that is a combined effort, students and staff.'

The two student newspapers, the *Isis* and the *Cherwell*, are entirely a student concern. They are newspapers; they report the news. They print interviews with politicians and with dons. This is not to say that they are good newspapers, but it is important to draw the distinction between them and the magazines issued by the *Asta*, in Germany, and by the *Orur*, in Rome, which are nothing but the mouthpiece of the central organisations. At Oxford there is no central organisation, no student parliament. The Junior Common Room in each college deals with internal affairs. I have often thought that it is the decentralisation of Oxford that stimulates student activity.

Oxford is a political university. Characteristically it was the first university to introduce a political science course in England in the form of PPE. The newspapers reflect the general interest in the workings of the world, in student political movements, in the meetings of the famous Oxford debating society, the Oxford Union. Many of England's most famous politicians have taken part in the Union as undergraduates. Eminent present day politicians come and speak in the debates. Two years ago Bobby Kennedy addressed the Union. The Union does not follow any specific trend, nor are its presidents of the same political opinions. Tariq Ali, the so-called revolutionary leader in English student politics, was once a president, as was Douglas Hogg, the son of a former Conservative minister. The political clubs at Oxford also seem to be the springboard for future politicians. The leaders of all three Parties, the present Prime Minister, Harold Wilson, Edward Heath, leader of the Opposition, and Jeremy Thorpe, leader of the Liberal Party, went to Oxford, and all three were active members of the Labour, Conservative and Liberal groups.

As active as the political groups is OUDS, the Oxford University Dramatic Society, brought to popular attention by Richard Burton and Elizabeth Taylor, who made their film *Doctor Faustus* in Oxford with an OUDS supporting cast. But apart from OUDS every college has its own drama group.

The brother of a friend of mine, Kevin Pakenham, was founding a new magazine, called *Cover*. His advertising campaign, 'Take Cover', had spread throughout Oxford. It was to appear in the autumn. I read its articles in the following year. Mainly artistic, it was interesting and original and, by the end of the year, was selling several thousand copies. 'It was hard work, frantic, but great fun,' Kevin told me.

From Paul's digs we walked into the centre of Oxford, towards the beautiful façade of Christ Church. We turned under an arch and stood in the Christ Church quad. A huge lawn lay before us, bordered by steps and a wide pavement, that spread out to the low yellow buildings decorated with thin, delicate arches and lattice windows. Christ Church Cathedral rose above the impeccable quadrangle; water gurgled in the fountain in the centre of the jade green lawn; groups of tourists clustered like ants at the far corners of the quad, admiring the symmetry. Other solitary figures walked along the paths or sat in the beautiful, still surroundings.

We walked through the great courtyard into the adjoining quad. Tall white buildings and large windows looked on to a small lawn. Undergraduates sat in the window frames, feet dangling. One person was playing a guitar, another reading. We climbed five flights of stairs to the room of an old friend, Robert Cecil. He was out. We decided to wait in his room, cleared a pile of newspapers and books from his sofa and sat down. The door opened and Robert, tall and dark, with a warm, frank expression, appeared panting.

'Been to a tutorial,' he explained. 'All term either I or my tutor have been postponing tutorials.' He pointed to his desk. Notes were strewn beneath books. 'Can't see you on Monday, could you come on Tuesday at 12.30,' one message ran. 'The net result,' Robert complained, 'is that I've now got a tutorial every day this week, and for each one I've got to produce an essay.' He sighed and sank into a chair.

History books cluttered his room. 'Half of this work is incredibly dull. At Oxford they are always teaching you things that are good for you, mental discipline and all that, they forget that, when a subject bores you, you don't work.'

Andrew was the first to agree. For his preliminary examinations, he had twice failed a compulsory Latin paper, and spent most of his second term not studying history but learning Latin. A Fellow of Magdalen, A. J. P. Taylor, commented, 'It's a hurdle, they have to put some obstacles in your way.'

'A trained mind, that's what they want,' Piers von Simson, the son of Werner von Simson who had been so kind to me in Freiburg, told me. Piers, tall, very good looking and not unaware of the fact, had just been accepted by BBC2, the most cultural and experimental channel, which provides a very high standard of television. He had taken a degree in modern languages, in French and German. 'In the interview I was told that I had developed a process of thinking which equipped me for many different jobs. I was delighted with this information. I've learnt about French and German poets, now I can assist a television team in its enquiry into witchcraft in Cornwall.

Such are the joys of a trained mind ...'

The subject matter of a degree course in the Arts, or in Law, does not decide your career. Many friends saw the university in some sense as a breathing space. 'You work hard for a degree; you want to get a good one,' Piers told me, 'but you don't have to be thinking, Have I chosen the right subject, will this degree allow me to do what I want.'

To many business firms, to newspapers and television, it is immaterial whether a person has a degree in history, PPE, English or even Modern Greats. The mark matters more than the subject. This attitude is, I think, important. It gives Arts students a wider choice of jobs and more hope for an interesting career. In France, Germany and Italy it is one of the most serious problems, one of the chief causes of revolt, that the only future open to Arts students is a job as an underpaid teacher.

A week later I was back in Oxford. I set up a camp-bed in Nadine's room at St Hilda's. The weather had held and it was sunny. The college was peaceful and quiet. Immaculate lawns lead down to the river. Tennis courts overlook the water. I couldn't understand why Nadine didn't walk on the grass. 'You're fined if you do,' she explained. 'The petty rules at women's colleges send you mad,' she told me as we went into her small, but cheerful, room. 'Women's colleges are supervised by scouts. They are always on our side,' she said. 'You're not meant to leave Oxford more than one week-end a term, but the scout, if you have a chat with her, turns a blind eye to your empty room, "Have a nice time ducks," she says, as she catches you creeping out of the college, your suitcase in your hand.'

Nadine loved the summer term, and I could see why, as I spent the morning in her room and watched five young men dart in and out to ask her to come punting that afternoon, to have lunch, to eat strawberries and cream, or to go to a party in the evening.

'Don't judge Oxford by the summer,' Nadine warned. 'It's fun, but even so the atmosphere of a women's college is appallingly neurotic. The pressure of work is enormous throughout the eight week term,' she persisted. Most of the girls I knew at Oxford felt the same. Angela, with long blonde hair and blue eyes, a very pretty friend of my brother's, also found the atmosphere at Somerville depressing. She decided it was the fault of the women dons.

'They are much less worldly than men. They get really angry if you don't hand in your essay on time, and are constantly reminding you how lucky you are to be at Oxford, and it is your duty to justify your place.' (One out of two boys are accepted, only between one out of fifteen and one out of thirty girls get a place.) 'If you look overworked and exhausted they will reduce your next essay to some less comprehensive subject, they will tell you to be more organised with your work, but they still keep talking about work ... they can't get off the subject.' She envied her male colleagues. 'One friend of mine was overworking. He went to a tutorial not having done his essay, pale and nervous. His tutor told him that he should take his mind off his work. He took him off to a pub and they spent the hour drinking beer. I sometimes wish one of my dons would, on the rare occasions when I am strained and weary, take me off to eat an icecream!'

'Either it's too much work,' said Nadine, 'or the love affair is going badly, or there is no love affair. How I hated the first year,' she recalled, 'I thought I was living in some home for manic depressives' ... but the sun was shining and it was time to go for a punt. 'Come back in the winter and you'll find loneliness, neuroses and undiluted gloom.'

It was seven o'clock and the streets were full of undergraduates in dinner jackets and girls in long dresses. Again I was confronted by a porter, but this time he handed me over to a scout. I asked to see Walter Scott.

'Mr Scott, ah yes. You're his sister I've no doubt.' He chuckled and, as we walked up the stairs, told me, 'He keeps a dog here you know, chocolate coloured retriever. Moffkins. Not brown but chocolate coloured. Quite forbidden you know. But then Mr Scott he's a one.'

We arrived. The scout knocked. Silence. He knocked again. A sleepy voice shouted 'Come in'. The sitting-room was in chaos, books and records and cushions thrown everywhere. In his small bedroom Walter was half asleep. The scout peeked his head in the door, 'The Dean, sir,' he said. Walter sat up with a jerk and looked aghast. The scout laughed. 'Don't worry sir, it's only your sister.' Walter looked equally aghast. He doesn't like many of his relations. His curly black hair hung over his pale face. And, when he saw me, he still looked aghast. He is a strange person. His black eyes stared at me blankly.

'You did ask me to this dance,' I said.

He nodded. 'Been up all night. Cambridge ball. Only got back this afternoon. Feel ghastly.'

I left him to change. Outside in the college grounds huge tents had been set up. Coloured lanterns lined the walls; gay decorations and signs hung in the corridors which led down to the college cellars where psychedelic lights flashed to soul music. 'By kind permission of the Wardens and Fellows,' said the invitation and so it was. No one was going to sleep that night.

I sat on a stone step and waited and meditated on the condition of students at Oxford. Without a doubt they are lucky. The University treats them as individuals, they have a place, they belong. Undoubtedly they are privileged. Oxford is open only to those who qualify. Some egalitarians would have it that its facilities should be open either to all or none. But Oxford can give its particular brand of education to only a few. It would be pointless to withdraw a high standard from a minority in order to give a low standard to a majority.

I knew that at Oxford there must be just as much loneliness and unhappiness as at any university but, on the other hand, people were given such a chance to think and to express themselves; in work, because it is based on your personal opinion; and through any medium to which you are drawn, music, art, painting, writing or simply talking. For this reason the atmosphere seemed far less frustrated than in the universities I had seen in France and Italy.

The use of power and its moral justification is a question that interests students all over the world. Television has started everyone thinking sooner. Because of the blank opposition towards free political expression, students are resorting more and more to violence. (The riots following the killing of a student had been raging in West Berlin for several days.)

Coming from the Continent, where in the universities, politics dominates, in Oxford I felt a different force. There was an interest in experimenting with ways of expression and communication, an inclination towards research and thought for its own sake. To act a play was interesting, not because the acting was good, but because it was a personal effort to express an idea. Equally, political discussions did not have to end in a mass demonstration and a punch-up with the police, but went further towards the more profound understanding of an argument. Perhaps what I sensed, alongside the ceaseless activity, was a respect for tolerance and time.

Long John Baldry and the Bluesology, the Caribbean all-steel band, the Leeds City Bagpipes band. . . . We drank innumerable glasses of wine as we toured the rooms of Keble open to all friends. In the Pusey marquee, with its ultraviolet lights, I remember the pulsating beat of the Howling Wolves, the Idle Race and the Exception. Dawn broke at six and we moved on to the lawn and danced in the thin, white light of early morning. No one was going to ruin the Oxford summer term, and what I found so cheering was that no one did.

It was too late to go to an hotel, yet too early to leave. After a few embarrassing entrances into occupied bedrooms, I found an empty one at Keble and decided to sleep there. A few hours after I had sunk exhausted into the arms of Morpheus a humourless scout walked in. 'There's a girl in there,' I heard him scream. I was alone so I didn't see the problem but he was upset. I left quickly, hitching up my dress under a borrowed raincoat to avoid any explanations.

In daylight, and with that suddenly sober feeling that dulls and dispirits, I could see quite how ugly Keble was. A student was holding out a hat. 'For the Demolish Keble Society,' he cried. 'How do I join?' I asked. 'Donate and pledge to remove one brick a year from Keble.' The idea was excellent, but the execution needed a vastly accelerated time-table.

Walter drove me to my car. I couldn't remember where it was. I wasn't quite sure if I was in Oxford or London, and only when I met Nadine was I certain. She had just stepped off a punt and was still in her long dress. We both changed and before I left Nadine insisted that I have breakfast at George's. We went to the Oxford Market, a city of stalls and narrow passages under cover, down an alley off the High Street. The Saturday shoppers were out in force.

We sat down in a café where the smells of cheeses and fresh

fruit floated in and mixed with black tea and bacon. I didn't feel very well. But George's had a great atmosphere. Several undergraduates, some in gowns, most in jeans, sat silently at tables drinking coffee. We both stared at one solitary figure sitting motionless in front of us. Open before him he had a copy of Hobbe's *Leviathan*. He was reading intently, oblivious to the noise and clatter around him. I supposed that he was typically Oxford.

At the next table sat three bearded young men eating gargantuan plates of bacon, eggs and sausages. ' Of course, his later poetry is of much less interest, metaphysically speaking ' . . . ' He never had the same degree of inner perception ' . . . I looked at my watch. It was ten o'clock. How ludicrously affected! I was definitely not feeling well. Our sullen silence was interrupted by the arrival of a group of merry, barefooted musicians, friends of Nadine's.

' I threw a glass in the river,' said a girl with a gesture.

' Next time throw yourself in,' grunted a long-haired young man. They sat down beside us and, to my dismay, they wanted to start a conversation.

' At university?' the long-haired man began.

' Not yet,' I said, ' I'm going to London.'

' Oh,' he said with a tinge of disdain. 'Thousands of you, aren't there? Just numbers, that's all you'll be, a number.'

'Not much university life at London is there?' said the girl with bare feet sweetly.

Another member of the group interrupted, ' King's College, did you say? King's College, Cambridge, of course?'

' London,' I said sourly.

' London,' he laughed. ' Where's that, Tooting Bec or Shoreditch?'

' Not in the provinces,' I muttered and gulped the sweet tea.

8

London
October – December 1967

T H E time for observing was over. I was a bona fide student. The University was my University, its life, my life. There was the work and the fun and a third dimension that I didn't really understand until I felt it within myself. There is you, the emerging person. New ideals clash against conclusions taken for granted; your whole being is churning like cheese in a barrel as you try to find out who you are and what you believe in. It is not surprising that a university is not a calm community; how could it be when its members are in a state of mild delirium. Life is exhausting. It hits the heights of enthusiasm and the pit of depression. Ideas solidify like icing on a cake until the opposite point of view appears like a candle and melts down all that you thought you understood until once again you stand alone and unsure.

University life is a vacuum. The grants system removes immediate financial worry. The only commitments are lectures and essay classes; otherwise time is your own. Work consists of neat arguments and solutions, and it is easy to apply the same formula to present day problems—to develop theories that sound perfect because on paper you don't have to take other human beings into consideration. I can solve the world in a day if I ignore human temperament, if I deny other people the right to disagree, and if I refuse to accept compromise not only as a need but as a duty.

Television has had an immense effect on my generation. It has opened new vistas, aroused a great desire to learn, it has instructed and has made an extensive amount of knowledge available to everyone. It has also brought home to a protected generation the horrors of war, of starvation, of brutality. The screen appeals not to reason but to emotion, and in students, where feelings dominate, the reaction is strong, sometimes violent. Television creates movements; on its wings it carries the student revolt throughout the world. At the same time it has stripped royalty and statesmen of their glamour. The world is in your sitting room; everywhere you see people, just ordinary people who are thinking, acting or influencing in a way that may change the world. To see men in action can inspire others, to watch a man on a screen as he tries to persuade you of an idea can be equally stimulating. I believe television is an activating force and has increased the individual sense of responsibility. There is a new restlessness in the air, particularly in England where the future seems so uncertain; the green isle has not dropped anchor, it is adrift. It is important to do something positive, to establish yourself as an individual. Young people are exploding with new ideas, with energy, with a creative force, but the blast is contained within a bubble of insularity.

Psychiatrists can adumbrate the stresses and strains of our times; they get it wrong. I am a stress and a strain to myself. If you try to rationalise me I think I shall scream; I know the essential about myself : I am confused.

I was a Fresher. That's what they told me. And as a Fresher I found King's College, London University, imposing. The old grey buildings stand beside Somerset House, where the population of England is registered, overlooking the murky green Thames. The front of the college, under massive reconstruction, faces the Strand. To one side lies Fleet Street and the Law Courts, to the other Nelson's Column and Trafalgar Square. The college borders on the City of London and a business air hangs above the high scaffolding which, so we are told, will one day be replaced by a glistening new building.

Liz was my Fresher mother. It was an unbelievable title. She was a second year history student, commandeered to give me a conducted tour round the buildings. Liz was thin and pretty and became a great friend, though initially I was so averse to the idea of having a Fresher mother that I wasn't very receptive. We visited the Chesham building, which used to be an hotel, and now houses the Union, the student parliament, and is officially the Union building. The refectory is one of the canteens in

King's. The Chesham was, and still is, notoriously drab, but I liked the atmosphere drawn from yoghourts and cigarette smoke. In the bar in the basement the juke box blared while pints of frothing beer spilled onto the low tables. I went on a tour of the mini-football and the darts room, to the indoor shooting range, to the discovery bar, grimmer and more lifeless than the Chesham. The notice boards were full of bright announcements calling Freshers to receptions, to folk concerts, to wine and cheese parties.

Then it was time for a pep talk by the Principal, who told us how lucky we were to be at King's, what an exciting three years it was going to be. We needn't work all the time but should take a healthy interest in the life of our most lively college . . . . Do something constructive like joining a club. And, of course, we shouldn't ignore our health. Anyone who felt sick was to see the college doctor, and if he wasn't around, some medical student. Sooner dead was my reaction, than be the guinea pig for some specimen-starved student . . . and . . . the voice droned on . . . be sure to walk to college. You must be joking was the silent unanimous thought of seven hundred freshers crowded into the main hall. London is a gargantuan city. The boy next to me muttered, ' I live in Balham. I came here to study not to train to be a long distance walker. . . .'

On the first floor of the college I discovered the general library and the Chapel. The King's Singers were practising in the high-ceilinged gilded room. King's was founded in 1829 with six Faculties of Arts and a Theological Department with the Chapel as its centre. I had noticed that theologians were everywhere in dog collars, in the Chesham and the bar, and had seen the Chaplain, an amusing and friendly man, in one of the common rooms where I went to read the newspapers.

Three thousand students, including post graduates, belonged to King's and I knew one. And Liz had lost herself in the streams of people that filed along the corridors. Everyone seemed to be saying hello to everyone else. I had not a thing to do and not a thing to say to anyone, and I began to resent these maddeningly busy people. I went home and watched television : Tom and Jerry Cartoons and the *Man from Uncle*. I even listened to the advertisements.

The bewilderment and loneliness of the first weeks passed

slowly as we, in our first year, began to know each other. The atmosphere was relaxed and intimate, more so I was told than in the other colleges of London University concentrated near Senate House and University College, in the drab surroundings of Goodge Street and the Tottenham Court Road. I soon realised that in England, students have a different conception of their universities. Ned, a crazy friend, with reddish hair and a brown beard, always dressed in khaki jacket and trousers, said with satisfaction as we filed into our first lecture, 'They've got us here for three years.' He was right. The selection for university had taken place and we were relieved of the immense burden felt throughout Europe of being thrown out after failing an examination, or at least being made to re-sit the examination again at the end of the following year. The end of the year examinations, 'sessionals', are guidelines at King's by which each person can judge his work. They are not aimed, as they are in France, at weeding out half the first year students.

In England universities select students before they come to the university, not during their courses. Each school-leaver can apply to six universities of his choice in order of preference, for a place in a particular faculty—arts, science, medicine—to study the subject of his choice : for instance history or a mixed course, depending on the university. Each application is considered in the light of the final schools examinations, 'A' levels, and then the aspirant students, quaking in their shoes, are called up for an interview at which the final decision is made. Over half the school-leavers who apply for a university place are refused admission. Some go to technical colleges, others get a job.

For those who are accepted, the three years at university are spent more or less free from the fear of being thrown out. It is a great advantage to feel installed in a university, to feel that you belong there, and that your teachers are not conducting some elimination game, forcing you either to leave or to repeat a year. If anyone fails an examination they are asked to take it again. If they fail for a second time, they might be asked to leave, although few people fail twice. The personal teaching methods, the close surveillance and the individual attention keep almost everyone up to the required standard to get a degree, and most students in England finish the course. What kind of degree a student gets depends, of course, on the amount he works. Only five per cent of students in any subject are awarded a first class degree. The other awards are a second class degree, divided into a two (one) and a two (two), and a third class degree. (The fourth has been abolished in most universities). It is an interesting point that although England has numerically far fewer students than, say, France, the actual number of graduates is almost the same, because of the very high proportion of English students who actually finish their degree course.

The British university system hinges on pre-university selection. Contact between students and their teachers in an essay class, where one teacher talks only to two students, is possible only among small numbers. Also the selective system makes it possible for the government to allot grants which, compared with European universities, are phenomenal. They are graded according to parental income and the maximum is three hundred and seventy pounds a year for Oxford, Cambridge and London, three hundred and forty pounds for other universities. Every student can claim a minimum grant of forty-eight pounds. The fact that any person accepted by a university is assured of enough money to live on during the term affects the general attitude towards education.

A friend at King's who came from a Welsh mining background explained, ' I knew I would get a grant if I got accepted by a university, so I really worked, and was encouraged by my family throughout my school years.'

From the first day at King's, though completely lost and glum, I was treated as an individual who needed help and advice. The staff of the History Department helped all Freshers choose their syllabuses. The Tutor to Women Students saw each new girl and tried to make her feel at home. Though nothing could alleviate the confusion it meant a great deal to know that the teachers saw me as a person and not as a number.

In the first week at the University I chose my curriculum. The choice was wide; the language barrier barred me from Asian, Oriental, African and ancient Greek history. I settled for European history which automatically includes a course in Political Thought. English history from 1066 to 1945 was obligatory, but European history of the same dates was divided into four sections and we each chose two. Dr Brown, the eminent medieval historian, who wears a cape, sometimes carries a cane, has a very dry wit and whose book on castles is definitive, tried to save historical souls from the temptation of the Modern Era. However, most of us chose to study European history from 1500 to 1945.

I was certain of my choice. Television, which has been in my life since I could turn the knobs, has given me a sense of urgency. I have less patience for the distant past. I wanted to learn something that is immediate and associable with present times. And I am allowed to. The University has evolved original and varied curricula. Also for the two more specialised aspects of the history degree course, the Optional and Special Subjects, I could choose from a list the subject and period that most interested me.

The choice of courses in English universities is enormous. The universities have a far greater degree of autonomy than in Italy, where they are under the thumb of the Ministry of Education. In Germany the *Land* government takes important decisions; in France before May 1968 the Ministry of Education had complete power; official permission was needed even to get a new chair. English universities have the power to select students, to establish a constitution, to devise their own curricula and to run themselves.

The degree courses at universities are divided between the one-subject degrees in the tradition of Oxford and Cambridge, and between the 'mixed courses' inherited from America. As a student I have the choice. If I feel that I want to study one subject for three (or sometimes four) years, I can apply to London, Oxford, Cambridge and many other universities which offer a more specialised degree course. (This isn't to say that I'll get in. At Oxford and Cambridge competition is phenomenal, and at London only slightly less acute.)

I wanted to study history for three years, and nothing but history. It is what interests me most at the moment, and I want to take the least superficial course. I am well aware that history is a mammoth subject. In three years I can only hope to scratch beneath the surface, (there is no question of going into depth as so many students at Oxford claim) but I need every moment of three years to do even that. There is also a philosophy behind the one-subject degrees.

'It trains your mind to cope with any situation,' was a remark of one teacher who had studied at Oxford. The idea, I think, is that for three years the students study one subject from as many angles as possible: I relate and inter-relate; I assimilate and digest knowledge and (hopefully) produce a cogent argument. And, lo and behold, the net result should be that I, with my trained mind, am equipped to run a scrap iron works, to become a cook or take over a Chinese laundry.

Sussex, a 'television' university, made a major breakthrough when it introduced a curriculum that deals in 'fields of study'. Sussex responded to the need felt by many students for a broader course that would equip people with more knowledge, and would be of more use generally. 'Not everyone wishes to be a teacher nor have their mind trained by *Beowulf*,' a friend at Bristol remarked. The Sussex curriculum is based on a concept of Modern Greats. The Greats course at Oxford covers language, literature, history and the philosophy of Greece and Rome, and follows the development of thought to the present day. This 'comprehensive course' has been re-instated at Sussex in its modern form. One of my friends had chosen European Studies. It is a four-year course, one of which must be spent in Europe. For her degree she must sit examinations in one modern language, in philosophy, in literature and in the history of one century of her choosing. She can choose a major subject; Kay chose philosophy. However, in the marking of examinations no distinction is made between major and minor subjects. Kay's history paper is marked as severely as if she were a history major, even though she has spent far less time, and had been given fewer lessons on history than in her major subject. But the examination system, Kay considered, maintains a higher standard.

The examination papers are exacting but they fit into the pattern of English education. For English 'A' level, taken at seventeen or eighteen, we were asked in forty minutes to write an essay on the use of the metaphor in literature. For the Oxford and Cambridge entrance exams the modern language papers asked for a comment on 'Goethe's university'. In the general literature paper for finals at Sussex the typical question topics are: 'Art is useless', 'Art no longer concerns the masses', 'Art is a product of the neurosis (Freud)'. The examination paper on 'the modern European mind', a course followed by all students of the European school, included questions on Freud, Nietzsche,

Kafka. Another paper, 'European foundations', covers much the same syllabus as my own course on political thought, Plato, Aristotle, Dante, Aquinas, Machiavelli.

The chief criticism of the 'mixed course' is that it is too superficial. Dr James told me that at York students who began a mixed degree course were changing to a specialised course, which they found more satisfying because they could concentrate on the subject that really interested them. A.J.P. Taylor is strongly opposed to mixed courses in a university. He would like to see a university a place of study only for first-class brains. 'Universities should be centres of research, and they should train teachers and specialists.' The majority of students want a more general education which, he feels, should be given by other institutions, by technical colleges or schools for higher education. Mr Taylor feels that all mixed courses are hopelessly superficial. 'As it is,' he told me, 'the history school at Oxford educates people to become good readers of the *New Statesman*, that is all.'

I have never taken a mixed degree course and cannot judge whether they are more or less superficial than my own degree course. Kay was adamant. At Sussex students worked extremely hard, read extensively and were no more superficial in their studies than at any other university. Certainly the students I have met at Sussex have been highly intelligent and extremely well-informed. Kay is delighted with her course, I with mine. Another friend went to Bristol to study law—one of the best courses in England. He too is satisfied. Though many friends at Oxford complain of the outdated syllabus, the strictly required reading lists, the *Beowulf* and the Latin, on the whole the student friends I have in England enjoy their studies because between them the universities can offer a wide choice of subjects. In France, Germany and Italy the fact that the curricula do not satisfy students at all is one of the major causes of unrest. As a student in England I count myself very lucky in this respect.

I was late for the weekly essay class. In the small office Ned lounged in a chair looking amused. The teacher, a charming young man with thick black hair, scowled. Five minutes before he had exclaimed, 'Where is the damned woman?' Here I was, muttering excuses. 'I met this old lady . . . she told me that she had just spoken to Our Lord . . . she had visited Him Up There.

She was going to become His wife and together they would run the Universe . . . I was so fascinated that when I looked up, lo and behold, I was in Gordon Square . . .' The teacher said he quite understood and I sat down exhausted.

For the first term we were three, Ned, myself and John, tall with curly black hair and a huge smile. John was a Lenin lover, which I discovered as soon as I read my essay on 'Account for the outbreak of the Russian revolution' (I had one a fortnight to write, now it is one, even two, a week). I had finished it at six that morning. Throughout the week I had spent several hours in libraries reading and taking notes.

Books are the source of information for an essay. A lecture is complementary but in no sense a substitute for personal research. The information is in a sense second-hand. The facts and opinions I produce for an essay are those of other historians. I am not (usually) in a position to produce original thought, nor do I see any original documents except in the Special Subject that I study in my third year. Inevitably my study is superficial. However, it is less superficial when the basis of my research is the work of great historians than when it is merely the digested content of a lecture. A book penetrates deep into a subject, lays out complicated arguments and conflicting views, but it leaves me and not the professor to do the job of thinking. I had to pick out the salient points of several books, to present an argument in the light of all the facts I had been able to collect and then to draw my own conclusions. Of course they weren't my own. Nevertheless I had, or thought I had, exercised my critical judgement. I had been given the freedom to choose what information I wished to use and which opinion I wish to endorse and in choosing I had thought for myself. This, I contest, is the most valuable aspect of education. It more than justifies a system based on individual research and is a testimony against the spoon-feeding that I had experienced in Aix.

The most important part of the whole process of writing essays is that you have fun. Mostly you can choose your essay subject. I asked specially for the Russian revolution. I was free to write whatever I liked. I could agree with the great historians, or disagree. My essay, which was deplorable, was judged not on the opinions offered but on the construction of the argument. If the ideas had been clearly and logically presented, I am told, I would have been given a higher mark. I felt oddly powerful when I sat down to give my interpretation of the subject. I knew that someone with extensive historical knowledge was going to read what I wrote and (incredibly enough) take it seriously. Under these circumstances studying was interesting, even enjoyable.

After I had read the essay aloud, and after the teacher handed it back to me the following week, I was inclined to think that he had taken it too seriously. His criticism had been gentle during the class and had provoked a general discussion about pre-revolutionary conditions in Russia. However, I now saw my essay covered in red pen marks. There was a series of exclamation marks beside my literary conclusion, drawn from Shakespeare, a universal source rather like the Bible. I had quoted from Horatio's speech at the end of Act 5:

                    so shall you hear
Of carnal, bloody, and unnatural acts;
Of accidental judgements, casual slaughters.

And things got worse. Ned was talking of Prussia and the Junkers. I said I thought that Junkers were like Middle West farmers. 'Why?' asked the teacher. I didn't know, well, on the other hand I did, it was sort of intuitive. Now that really was a faux pas. 'Intuition,' boomed the otherwise calm teacher, 'I must have historical evidence Miss Crawley, not intuition, above all not feminine intuition!' He banged his fist on the table. John and Ned sat back and gloated. I was delighted when soon after it was time to leave. All the same, the hour had been fun. I had had the chance to ask the questions that had puzzled me when writing my essay. I had listened to the teacher's point of view as he gave us all the benefit of his greater knowledge. He had answered our questions and discussed them openly, yet he always allowed us the right to our own opinion. He did not try to dissuade us from our conclusions, even though he disagreed, as he did with John over Lenin. We, as individuals, were free to think what we liked. I had not studied history since I was thirteen. I could truthfully say I knew nothing about it, and I felt even more the privilege, not only of this direct conversation with a teacher, but also his respect for his most junior students.

We went to the Chesham. It was lunch time in late November, the canteen was packed and I queued with Ned. He bought a sandwich, I a yoghourt. Like most of my friends Ned never ate lunch. The grant goes far but not that far, and it is easy to economise on food. We sat down at a table scattered with cheese and crisps. Paul, bespectacled and highly intelligent and like Ned a specialist in military history, sat beside Sue Fremlin, a small, pretty girl with long black hair. She had just come from the library where she had been working on an excruciating essay on the increase of coal production during the industrial revolution. We were all first year history students. I was almost the only person in my year to come from London. My friends came from all parts of England. They lived either in the halls of residence in Clapham, Mitcham, London suburbs, or more centrally near Senate House, or they shared a flat, or had digs. Sue, a Catholic, was in the charge of nuns who ran a Catholic school.

I was quietly eating my yoghourt when Ned, having gulped down a plastic cup of boiling coffee, stood bolt upright, dramatically threw out his hand and cried, 'Good-bye friends.' He ripped off his brown jacket to reveal the top of a naval uniform and rushed out of the door. Sue explained that he was part-time sailor on board a ship moored just outside the college. At one o'clock the whistle blew and he had to be aboard, standing to attention and saluting. From the window I watched him running down the street in the direction of the Embankment.

He only just missed Richard, who emerged from the room next door to the canteen, where students lay in chairs, sat on the floor and talked or stared through the smoke-filled air at the television. With books under his arm and a guitar slung over his shoulder, Richard wandered up to our table. His long blond hair hung over his spectacles. He was tall and rake thin, and had on blue jeans worn at the knees and covered in patches. On the table he placed his pile of books. They were all in German: biographies of Goethe, Schiller, Bismarck, Hitler, Frederick the Great. He loved the German language and literature and was fascinated by its history. At the end of the year he answered the whole of the European history paper on Germany alone. Perspicaciously the examiner wrote at the bottom, 'You seem to have a marked preference for German history.' But since he got very good results no one complained.

We didn't have time to cross the street to the pub. It was time
for a lecture. The room was full though not overcrowded.
Seventy students sat along the benches, leaving many empty
places. Dr Brown was discussing King John. That he was an
expert on his subject no one doubted, but in spite of his extensive knowledge he was not dogmatic. He stated repeatedly that
he was giving his own opinion, and even though I, for one,
knew absolutely nothing about King John, I still had the right
to differ. All lecturers stressed that a lecture was a point of
view. I was very struck by this. It was a tone that I had not
heard anywhere else in Europe. In Rome, Paris, even Berlin,
lectures were regarded as a source of knowledge, and the lecturer seen more as the giver of knowledge than as the defender
of an opinion. At King's I often heard the remark, ' Now
when you study the subject you may disagree with this . . .'
I felt a marvellous sense of freedom. No one was trying
to shove an opinion down my throat; I could draw my own
conclusions.

It is a freedom that as an English student I am used to. It
begins at school, in preparing for the final 'A' level examinations taken in two or three subjects. At fifteen or sixteen, you
begin to think for yourself, to use reference books, to read
criticisms. In history you study the background works and whatever more specialised books you have time for. Work for 'A'
level is accepted in America as the equivalent to the first year
at university. At one of the nine schools I went to, a day school
in London, I was initiated into individual research at the age
of twelve. For one term we each had to write a 'book' on the
reign of Elizabeth I. We could obtain information where we
liked. My source was a picture history of England. It was the
most exciting term of my life. I spent hours reading about Eliza-
bethan architecture, clothes and furniture, listing Shakespeare's
plays, drawing pictures of the Globe Theatre, reading Gren-
ville's poem 'The Revenge', learning about Drake and the
Armada. We were taken to museums and art galleries, to Hamp-
ton Court and Hatfield, two of Elizabeth's royal residences. To
this day I remember much of what I wrote then. At times I got
carried away. I was writing about houses and sanitary conditions
and the Plague. I illustrated my text by a picture of a crowd,
many heads and hats drawn in bright colours. The caption read,

'In a crowd like this you can see that plague and disease could easily spread ...'

The whole of university life works on a basis of co-operation between students and their teachers. The King's Union, the student parliament, administers a budget of fifteen thousand pounds a year with the help and advice of some of the staff. The National Union of Students held discussions throughout last year with the Government, demanding an increase in the grants. A rise was obtained, not enough, but something.

Whatever the formal definition of a democracy, at the heart of it must lie the ideas of the citizens who participate as fully as their abilities allow them to do and of decisions that are reached after discussions.

Over the last few years there has been a move in many universities to have greater student representation. In Sussex the radical student demands for representation at all levels were met completely and, as my friend at Sussex told me, most students are satisfied with the way the University is managed. At Bournemouth the same type of reform took place. Somerville College, Oxford, is discussing a system that will bring students and dons closer together, and will give students a greater say in their own affairs. At the London School of Economics problems of discipline and overcrowding have led to radical demands for student power which are not likely to die down. In most universities the old university set-up, where teachers were in loco parentis, has died. Students want more responsibility, and it is one of the greatest strengths of the English educational system that university teachers and professors are not a remote authoritarian body but are willing to listen and to accept change.

I was sitting at the back of the Large Lecture Theatre. It looked like a Greek stage. Rows of curved benches descended steeply to the stage below. I had squeezed into the hall the week before when a minister had given up his lunch hour to make his way from the Houses of Parliament along the Embankment to King's where he addressed a packed hall. Many politicians, at the invitation of the political clubs, emerged from those neo-Gothic buildings to enlighten the inmates of King's.

The turn-out for the debates is organised by the Law Faculty once a week, so that future barristers can give us a taste of rhetoric. Debating is highly organised in English universities. There are debating teams and competitions. The procedure is formal, as in a House of Commons debate; the speeches can be quite funny. The motion for this debate was 'This house believes that marriage is an out-of-date institution'. The engineers packed the back of the hall, shouting and whistling as they always do. Marriage didn't secure stability ... if you didn't believe in the sanctity of marriage then why marry ... arguments and quotations were thrown at the assembly. Beside me a boy rose and said that if you didn't have marriage you would have large-scale perversion ... And what about the children, asked a girl from the other side of the hall. If there is no marriage who will care for the kiddies ... Lump them all in a communal home, said another boy, and let's go back to Plato.

My thoughts wandered. I stared at the faces along the brown benches. Beards, spectacles, intense eyes and interesting expressions, yet I knew not a soul. How could I meet other people? The question was pathetic yet quite real. In lectures and essay classes I only met first year history students. I knew no one in their second year, and as for people studying other subjects, law, English or languages, they were in another world. I was at an initial disadvantage living at home: friends who lived in halls of residence came in contact with students in all faculties. The college tried to make first year students take part in its life; there were parties for Freshers, there were folk concerts in the evening. But do you hang around by yourself and go alone? I didn't want to. Yet I envied everyone who had someone to talk to. I had many ideas and I wanted to communicate. At times I felt such a prisoner in my isolation that I had to force myself to set foot in King's.

Most friends who have been to university know what it's like, to feel alone when surrounded by hundreds of people. I don't think anything can prevent the feeling of being totally apart. To make a friend takes hours of discussion and a great deal of effort. At King's second year students took no interest in the Freshers. We were left to fend for ourselves. We all wanted to make as many friends as quickly as possible, to get the effort over, and everyone became knotted up in the attempt, and sank into a state of exhaustion and dullness. At university there is nothing except work or communication with other people. A student has no job, no occupation; he studies and broods. Some days I came to King's hoping to meet a familiar face. I longed to speak to someone in the college. I found hundreds of prohibitive human frames bustling through corridors, ignoring me completely.

'Now why don't you speak to me?' I shouted out in my mind to the good looking boy who was picking out a huge sausage roll in the canteen. But he says nothing, he pays, the till rings its tiny bell and he loses himself in the tables and chairs. And me, well I decided to walk home through St James's Park, to look at the pelicans, watch children feed the birds and meditate on how utterly disappointing it is to be a student.

I had London to console me. It is an extraordinary city. Nowhere do I feel so free. I can leave the house looking worse than Dracula, which I often do, barefoot and dishevelled, and no one so much as stares. For me London is a city without formality or convention. You can dress and behave as the fancy takes you.

For my friends who were strangers to London as well as to King's the first months of university were gloomy days of rain and loneliness. Kate, a tall pretty girl with short red hair, a direct manner, and a striking way of using words, remembered the first weeks in London. 'Grey houses, cross traffic wardens, ugly buildings and long empty week-ends with no one to visit. Nothing to do but walk for several hours in Hyde Park, watch children float their boats on the Round Pond and kick the damp autumn leaves.'

Gradually each of us came out of hibernation. My friends gave up their more respectable clothes for trendy gear. Sue cut six inches off her hem, Kate wore bangles and beads, Ned took to a Maverick tie, John appeared in psychedelic shirts and flowered ties and Patsy appeared in leather boots and a maxiskirt. Everyone's hair grew longer. The London Look had conquered, just in time for a commemoration week, for the series of dances, 'hops', folk concerts, and (less monotonous) performances of *Troilus and Cressida* by the Drama Club. There was a visit to LUDS (London University Dramatic Society) Senate House Theatre to see a play of which I could stand only one act, and a rowdy Union meeting in the large lecture theatre, where several people lost their shirts, which brought the first term to a noisy close.

Some of the isolation had gone. It was time to talk. With John I had long discussions about Lenin and Stalin over a yoghourt in the Chesham. Richard and I spent a Sunday afternoon in St James's Park watching the pelicans and talking about Mann. Ned held forth on pantheism, Sue on Roman Catholicism, a theologian friend on the out-dated concept of celibacy for Roman Catholic priests. Friends began to come to my house and we sat up half the night discussing modern art and the value of pop culture and that favourite subject, how do you define art? I realised that I was beginning my education. On the one hand were the reform movements of the thirteenth century, on the other the problems of the modern world. Knowledge and thought were exciting. Everywhere I turned I found stimulating people, fermenting with ideas; young people who were groping like me for some answers.

My friends had discovered the potential of London. There were museums and art galleries to visit, plays and concerts to hear. At night student parties took us to all corners of London. My car bulged with eight squashed bodies, that is until the constable in Belgrave Square whistled to me to stop. Would I mind releasing half my passengers, he politely asked, then I might be able to see in my mirror, to change gear and perhaps even steer.

At King's also there were things to do. I had written an article for the *King's News*, the college paper. Like the *Cherwell* it is a newspaper and prints opinions and views. It takes a stand and is nobody's stooge. John became Vice-President of the Labour Club. Patsy was head of a national Young Catholic organisation. Ned ran *War on Want* lunches throughout the term, and later in the year was elected convener of debates. Sue became a General Representative, a minor Union official. And Dick, well Dick played soccer. Dick had tousled yellow hair, a square face, was tall and very strong. And on Thursdays he limped, because, he explained, on Wednesdays he played soccer and his boots were too tight and they hurt his feet. So, on Thursdays he limped. We all knew, as we do now, that King's is a closed world. But it offers time to think and this is a great luxury.

It was raining hard. We ran across the Strand and caught the bus up the Aldwych to Senate House, where some of the most eminent professors gave open history lectures. The hall was full. I had that contented feeling that I was in the process of being instructed.

At the end of the hour nuns, students, middle-aged men and women spilled out of the doors. Kate, in her shorter-than-ever green dress, invited me for a cup of coffee in her room. The students' residence building stood across the street. Other residential halls were scattered throughout London. Kate's room was small and neat; she shared it with another girl. 'I get on very well with my flatmate,' she explained in her direct manner, 'but sometimes I long to be alone.' Many of her friends in the same building had a room to themselves. Posters of London were pinned to the walls: the Houses of Parliament and behind them a sunset.

Kate produced a biscuit tin and we sat and talked. Kate spoke in rather unusual language – 'such is the way of the world', 'not its most important propensity' – she had a clear face and a distant expression in her eyes. She had felt acutely the loneliness of the University and of London; she knew what an effort it was to make friends. 'You have to fight, and all the while there is a smugness in people's eyes saying, there's a Fresher, she wants to make friends. I don't have to. They did, when they first came, but they forget that ... They leave us to face the vice of this great city all alone,' she sighed. But she meant it. More than the work, and the loneliness, Kate found the moral confusion the worst. 'You have to work out for yourself where you stand,' she said, 'there is no doubt about it, women are equal to men. First it was the vote and now it's the pill. We live in a new era of freedom.'

'All this sophisticated talk about sex is a load of rubbish. Girls aren't cynics; it isn't inevitable that you sleep with the person you go out with. When you are independent for the first time, as we are here, a love affair is tremendously important. If you sleep with someone it means a great deal.'

I was sitting in my orange basement when a friend visited me. She worked in London. Like many friends she had lived in a flat by herself since she was eighteen. She was very direct. 'Let's face it sex is fun. The pill unknots these inhibitions, all this morality handed down from one's parents. You don't become callous, just more realistic. You see sex in perspective. It's part of a normal relationship.'

In the basement of King's John had spilt the beer over the table; he went to get a rag. Next door in the bar Ned was putting sixpences into the juke box. Welsh folk songs, a jig and bagpipes wailed in the air. I was sitting with Patsy and another friend, Mary, in her second year in English, eating crisps. 'Romance is dead,' sighed Patsy. Her various boy-friends were forever making pilgrimages to London. 'In London these crazy girls think they have to sleep with a boy before they can become his friend. Sex precedes emotion,' she said with despair. I wasn't so sure. It depends on you. Personally I don't feel like Mrs Robinson, Pussy Galore, or The Callous Heroine in *Les Liaisons Dangereuses*. Admittedly where Patsy had a point was in the approach of most men. No long walks by the Thames, no strolls in a park, no 'Caves', no visits to the theatre, intimate nightclubs, just a dinner loaded with wine, followed by passes in a car, and the inevitable invitation to have a cup of coffee at three in the morning.

Mary was more optimistic than Patsy. 'Morals haven't changed. Most girls don't sleep with men for whom they don't feel a strong affection if not love. And many girls at university don't sleep with anyone at all.' She discounted the promiscuous swinging London set. 'They are bad at conversation and have a purely physical imagination.'

Undoubtedly the pill frees a girl from living according to generalisations like, 'don't sleep with a man before you marry, you might get pregnant'. But I don't think it changes anyone's character. If you are going to be promiscuous you would be without the pill; for most people sex is part of love and without love it means nothing.

Kate arrived in a black cape and leather boots. 'Morality means integrity. Don't betray your feelings nor misuse other people's. Let your conscience be your guide,' she said solemnly. 'And if my conscience sides with my passion when I think it ought to side with my reason, is it my conscience?' Patsy asked. 'Aye, there's the rub,' Kate admitted as she went to fetch a sausage roll.

Ned appeared. He had run out of sixpences. Generally sex

wasn't discussed much. People were not prudes, just discreet. However, Ned offered his view, as a Roman Catholic. 'Saint Augustine did a great disservice in giving to sex a sinful connotation.' He added dryly, 'It was all right for him; he had had his fling by then.' Like most of my Roman Catholic friends, Ned felt that to sleep with someone you are in love with is a natural part of the relationship. The Pope's encyclical came as a huge disappointment. 'It has ignored the crying needs of the world for the sake of a bigoted argument,' was one opinion. A girl remarked, 'The Catholic Church is failing to establish an acceptable code of life.'

A code – is that what we are after?

9

London-Oxford
January – April 1968

AFTER Christmas when the streets of London gave up their bright decorations, when sale notices replaced baubles and sparkling Christmas trees in the shop windows, when the rain fell in steady grey drops, millions upon millions from the thick sky, when fog and mist coated the grey buildings, the atmosphere turned stale. London is never a depressing city to me. I feel part of its moods, I love to breathe the smog and dirt, to feel that I'm rotting in the claustrophobic, used air. However, I knew that my friends found the city dejected; even the Thames had turned sour. And during the wet winter months the city had swallowed the University. At King's nothing seemed to be happening. All those clubs and societies that had accosted Freshers at the beginning of the year had gone underground. There was only the occasional film, a visit from an MP, but everyone was saying how dead it all was which made it even worse. Lectures followed essay classes and drinks in the pub and fewer laughs. Little cliques wandered through King's exchanging jokes that only they could understand, or couples walked hand in hand, while most first year students, neither in cliques nor hand in hand, were left to feel dispirited. A new series of personal problems were beginning for everyone.

First, the organisation of the history course and much of its teaching came under criticism. There are good tutors and bad tutors and I suppose each university has its share. To have an essay class, the kernel of your university education, with an uninteresting man is dissappointing to say the least. However, each term you have a different teacher. Personally I was totally dissatisfied with the lectures, so much so that after the first term

I went to one out of four a week, and sometimes not at all. I was relieved to find Richard and Ned doing the same. Most of the lectures were of little help, given, as it were, in a vacuum, bearing no relation to the essays we were doing. The interesting views put forward were lost on me, because I could not place them in any historical context. Too little was said about the important subjects, too much about obscure topics, and much that was said was very dull. Some of the teachers spoke openly against lectures. One told me, ' It's worth going only to take down the list of books for further reading at the end. Otherwise a lecture is a waste of time. You can get all the information in more concise and clear terms in a book.'

The teacher who said this to me was about the only lecturer whose lectures were packed because he was an interesting, provocative and informative speaker.

A disjointed syllabus, too few essays (only one a fortnight, which meant that no one felt prepared for the examinations at the end of the year), the usual dose of uninspired teaching, was the background to more acute personal problems. Old friendships were on the wane, new ones beginning. Kate had met a Sussex student, a crazy artist who sat up half the night mixing paints with egg yolks and browning. Andrew was looking for a new 'steady'. The loneliness of the vast city created an intense atmosphere.

Kate was reading a book in her room. Outside it was raining. ' I'm blue,' she said suddenly, 'life is such an effort at the moment.' Blues is a contagious disease. It comes with a debt, with a bust-up, with a rebuff, with rotten essay marks, with too much work, with a major crisis or a minor setback.

I met Richard as he wandered along the Aldwych. ' I should be studying German,' he sighed. ' I'm just not interested in the industrial revolution.'

Ned was sitting in his small room in the Commonwealth students' house off the Euston Road. From his window I could see a tree in the garden below. 'Each of us must have a cause to die for,' he said quietly. 'We can't live from day to day.'

Phœbe wandered through the corridors of King's. Vague and very pretty, her blue eyes looked sad. 'This is a ghastly place,' she muttered, ' the apathy is stifling.'

John was sitting alone in the history library. 'Just why do

I need a degree?' he pondered, 'For a job, I know. But what job? Some dreary nine-to-five office job.' He sighed. 'Emigration,' he muttered despairingly, 'emigration.'

I understood him perfectly. I had two friends recently married who hoped to emigrate to Australia as soon as possible. 50,000 people emigrate a year, many of them skilled people. And we are always hearing about the brain drain to America. 'It's all right for people with a vocation, for a writer, a painter, for a social worker, for a priest,' said a particularly disenchanted friend at King's, 'they know what they are going to do. Life has a point. Now I have no vocation. But for people who don't know what they're doing, like me, you must provide a few perks, like the chance to make some money if you work for it, the chance to give your children a higher standard of living than you had, and a better chance. As I see it, you work for nothing. This country hasn't any spark for the ordinary person.'

'England is bursting at the seams,' said a married friend who hopes to emigrate as soon as possible. 'Life would become more interesting for everyone if the energy of England were free to expand, if people who worked could earn more money, if industry were freer to expand, if this country could make people feel it was worthwhile to live here. Instead the young people, clever but poor, go to America or Australia. England needs a *raison d'être.*' Europe, I thought. Its future must be with Europe.

However, there are many little Englanders. For several student friends Sweden is the ideal. A marvellously run country with wonderful social services, schools and hospitals, self-sufficient, self-contained, isolated and neutral. England as a country is not neutral. My friends are not neutral, they are positive, with immense energy and a will to construct and to give. 'I know that the plight of old people in this country is acute,' said Jim, a lawyer, 'but I can't make this my cause. I need a cause but it must be a cause of ideals, fighting for a freedom, for a value, giving something to civilisation.'

For some, the real issue is equality. Whether egalitarianism means a decline in standards, whether it caters for the lowest common denominator and not for the highest, is a key question. However, neither I nor most of my friends at London seriously believe that people are equal, nor find anything altruistic in thinking they should be. 'What the hell does it mean?' Ned asked himself, as he put his feet on the table in his room. 'We don't look alike, we don't have the same thinking capacity, nor the same talents.' Ned was a Catholic. He believed that before the eyes of God men were equal. 'Since Marx people think that Man is God, and therefore change the philosophy to "in the eyes of the world men are equal". Is Miller as good a writer as Hemingway? Is everyone as good as everyone else? Is it just as good to be an omelette maker in the Golden Egg as it is to be a great musician? I'm not saying the omelette maker is not as good a human being; he may well be a far better person. But why not recognise that the great musician is giving more to civilisation than the omelette maker?'

'It's rubbish,' said one friend who came from a working-class background. 'I have worked fantastically hard throughout my school days to get to university. No one can tell me that I am the same as my friends at school who didn't do a stroke and wanted to leave school at fifteen and get a job. I'm not saying I am better than them – we chose to lead different lives. But I am saying that we are different. We are not equal.'

'The Government wants to be the parish priest,' said one friend caustically, and cited the Welfare State as the main example. I don't know whether the Welfare State takes the burden of responsibility away from the individual. Certainly, my American friends have a far more acute sense of social responsibility than friends in England. I don't know one person of my age in America who hasn't spent at least one summer doing social work, simply as part of his or her school programme. Many have gone on with social work at university. The individual is involved with the social problems of the State. In England, among students at any rate, I have found a different attitude. Many people feel exempted because the State has taken upon itself to be the social conscience.'

'The root of the trouble is this idea that the country owes you a living,' said a young journalist, Lynda Lee Potter, a forthright and attractive person. Lynda came from a poor family. She had worked tremendously hard and felt passionately that people in England should rid themselves of the idea that it was wrong to make money, however hard you tried. 'My husband is a doctor and we have both worked bloody hard all our lives, though we haven't a penny to show for it. Everything we earn seems to

be swallowed up in tax. I'll work, but I want a reward. Everyone else seems to think that they should get something without
effort.' She sympathised with student demands for a higher
grant. 'But they should remember that they are not the only
ones who need more money. It's time people realised that life
isn't a piece of cake, that you must struggle for what you earn.'
I felt she had a point though in principle I wholeheartedly support the Welfare State. Yet I know countless mopers and whiners,
unidealistic people who rot with resentment, whose only standard
is 'what I don't have, no one else shall have.' It is even more
depressing than the telephone system or British Railways.

The Marxist argument can sound very convincing on paper.
I was talking to one bearded friend at the LSE, a true Red.
I had long realised that for many people communism is a faith.
It is the new religion, and its advocates pursue the communist
ideal with the same blind vehemence that Roman Catholics
showed in the Inquisition. The line is, 'we are doing the best
thing for you. If you can't see it our way we'll have to suppress
you. But,' they say sweetly, 'don't forget that we are saving your
soul.'

And what about tolerance (which is not the same as indif-
ference), and human dignity and freedom of expression, and
freedom to live the life you want, to be your own moral arbiter?
Ah well, that is a problem. There is a Right and a Wrong, and
individuals must not contest this. And who decides on the Right
and the Wrong? The Party, until it becomes self-evident. No,
I wasn't with him. If I want to spend my life in Hyde Park,
that's my affair. You keep your Right and Wrong, I'll choose
my own thank you very much.

'The left is restless,' Graham Searle said ponderously, as he
sat cross-legged in a small union office in the Chesham at King's.
At that time he was president of the King's Union; later he was
Vice-President of the National Union of Students. 'They are
bitterly disappointed with Wilson. He isn't a socialist. He has
left the means of production in private hands. They accuse both
parties of being the same, capitalists, and focus their opposition
on the whole of society.'

It was a bad time of year. The late winter dragged on; the
parks were cold and the air bitter, while the watery sun held

back the spring. I went down to Oxford to find I don't know what. A new thought, a positive thought perhaps.

I hardly recognised the City of Spires. Sheets of rain fell over the windscreen of my car, I drove past Christchurch where even the beautiful yellow stones seemed grey, and arrived at Magdalen. I slipped past the porter's office and made my way to Andrew's room. I pushed open the door. The room was dimly lit by a small lamp, outside it was almost dark. Andrew sat on the floor, huddled in front of his electric fire, with a heavy book on his knee. The room was silent and dull. Andrew looked very tired. 'I've got to get through this entire book and then write an essay, all before tomorrow morning. I have two essays a week, and it's sending me mad. It's too much work. My tutor thinks so too, but there's nothing to be done. The syllabus must be finished. This is ruining the whole point of university.' Andrew was in a bad way. I left him in the Dickensian setting to make my way across the road to St Hilda's, where I was spending the night with Nadine, on a camp bed on her floor. It was very cold and the sharp air bit into my face.

In her room Nadine was working too. 'You are so lucky not to be here,' I heard her say as I was setting up the bed. I looked up in surprise. What had happened to Oxford? It was so easy to overwork, she explained. The thought of getting a good grade in Finals, the general pressure drove several of her friends to the libraries for eight hours a day. 'You work fanatically to do a good essay and as soon as you have finished you have another to do. It is easy to lose all sense of proportion and when you haven't done an essay, to despair.'

In the morning it was still raining. The streets were deserted. Outside Blackwell's I noticed bicycles propped up on the pavements. The river shimmered as its surface wrinkled with the fall of raindrops. The roads glistened. Figures scurried past, huddled under umbrellas. In the post office I met a boy I knew. We went to have some coffee in the market.

He also looked dejected. One of his friends had suffered a nervous breakdown and was now being treated in the Warnford, the psychiatric clinic at Oxford. The pressure of work, the enormous syllabus and the tense social life had been too much for him. His mind was swamped in confusion and worries and he was unable to write an essay. His tutors had shown him the greatest sympathy, and finally the President had advised him to go to the Warnford for treatment. He did not live there but was continuing his studies, under the supervision of medically qualified teachers, who helped him to cope with the problems that he had to face.

We watched the drops of rain run down the window pane. My friend was in his first year of law, sad and alone. He tried to explain how even in a college surrounded by people you could feel totally cut off. I more than understood. 'But in London, at least you can break away from university life and do something else,' he pleaded. 'Here there is only the cinema, and soon you have seen all the films and there is nothing to do but sit in your room by yourself.' He put his head in his hands. 'It is my own fault. I am my own prison, my own enemy. I can't break out of myself.'

Nadine had hated her first two terms at Oxford. 'It's not that people are unfriendly,' she tried to explain. 'It's this English regard for privacy. If you're sitting alone people think you want to be alone. On the contrary, you are probably longing to talk to someone.' I left in the rain. It was a delight to come into the bright lights of London, to see people fill the streets in spite of the weather.

With the spring, King's came to life. There were 'hops', balls, 'rave-ups' in the College when beer drinking contests spread among spectators, when the Chaplain was heard making coarse jokes, when satirical sketches attracted boos and wails from a drunken audience. Not last nor best was my rendezvous every lunchtime with Chris, a friend studying medicine. Chris and I had found ourselves representing London University in an insane skiing competition in Scotland, where it was considered 'cissy' to use a ski lift, and where gales and biting winds were tossed aside as not being worthy of notice. 'Up here, you'll find we're not fair weather skiers,' said one Scotswoman as she fought her way through a blizzard, her frozen family trailing behind her, to sit at the top of the mountain and have a picnic lunch. She wasn't even on skis. 'It's Sunday and I always take my family for a hike,' she explained. Her husband was up to his neck in a snow drift, crying for mercy. Chris, who ski'd in a night cap and red and black striped socks, was the centre of hilarity, and to my joy I found that he was a member of Kings. When the holiday was over I used to meet him in the smoke-filled room beside the bar, where with his Turkish friend Ishmail, he took on all comers at the greatest of all games: mini-football. It was a lunchtime treat.

Even Union meetings, those sombre affairs, became more amusing. The Union runs much of the college life. The finance committee deals with a budget of fifteen thousand pounds. The Union employs secretaries and provides each president with a sabbatical year. It is awarded grants for the different societies. The Chesham House standing committee deals with the Chesham, the refectory bar, and the Union shop, that sells a strange collection of things from stockings to note paper. There are committees for internal and external affairs. Every faculty elects a general representative who communicates with and assists Union officers. It does a lot of good work. It fought hard, together with the NUS, for the grants campaign. It helps organise and advertise student holidays and does a service in finding accommodation for students. Its Chairman of Entertainments takes over the commemoration week each autumn and organises the many dances throughout the year.

At the Union general meetings the different officers present their reports and we, the audience, who fill the benches of the Large Lecture Theatre vote on the minutes. In 'any other question' and 'question time' anyone can ask a question or make a proposal. The system is democratic, based on committees and sub-committees that submit everything to a general assembly. I was intrigued to remember that in Paris the committees set up during the revolution worked on almost exactly the same line as most English university unions. Criticisms of the Union are endless. Some claim it saps the college of enthusiasm, it is overbearing and an encumbrance, always demanding more paperwork than producing original ideas. Others feel it is stifled by bureaucracy, formalities and jargon, and it doesn't really pay heed to new ideas; it follows its own tradition and for every innovation offers automatic opposition. Ned and Paul would like to abolish the Union. Ned would like to abolish the King's constitution, but that is Ned . . .

I agree with many criticisms of the Union. Perhaps the severest condemnation is the low attendance at Union meetings, the low voting poll at elections (about one fifth of the college bothers to vote), and the general lack of interest. This is not so much the fault of the Union as of London. The city decentralises the College to a great degree and absorbs much of its energy.

I believe a central organisation is necessary. The people who work for it are specialists. They take on huge jobs of student accommodation, grants, and the endless complications of running the College. The result is that the Union is quite efficient. Many people dislike a centralised form of administration. One official said, ' There is no use suggesting some more direct form of participation in running the College unless a greater number of people are prepared to take on responsibility.' This, he maintained, was the key to the much wider question of direct management. ' At King's students are not interested enough in the management of the College; they take it for granted. Although many people object to the Union, few are prepared to take over the jobs of the Union officials.'

We all, Ned and Paul included, enjoyed the ' handing over' session, when the new union executive took over from the old. The Large Lecture Theatre was packed. Engineers stood at the back of the hall, shouting and whistling. The new 'general reps' were introduced. Amid cat-calls and screams the girls were made to stand up on the table while their legs and general appearance were scrutinised. The meeting got more and more rowdy. Sandbags were hurled down on to the platform and exploded in a cloud of dust. Suddenly a group of engineers thundered down the gangway and, hurling sandbags at the newly installed officers, dragged the President from his chair and ripped his trousers from him, to reveal a pair of leopard skin drawers.

The Chapel was the scene for some strange proceedings. Earlier in the term a theological play had been produced. Written by Ian Burgford it was about Adam and Eve after their ' interview' with God, which led to their expulsion from Paradise. Eve was capricious and feminine, Adam worried and pensive. The effect of the play was altogether hysterical, a sort of ecclesiastical Dick van Dyke show.

The folk festival also took place in the Chapel. Richard, with his guitar on his knee and a harmonica in his mouth, sang 'And he like she, and she like he' (a commentary on current fashions).

He wrote his own songs, and sang them with great humour, to the gilded ceiling and fat cherubims, to forty or so students, and to the silent theologians, who sat in a far corner of the Chapel, reading.

I stared up at the ceiling, at the stillness. We were so free. Richard could write songs and sing them. I could write awful poems and tear them up. Ned had his novel which he carried with him everywhere. He wrote in parks beneath the trees, he wrote in the countryside or in his small room. Paul spent nights at the opera; Ian invented his drunken Irish songs. We each had our own world, unfettered by any prescribed way of life. No hours, no rules, no conventions, just us, what we thought and what we wanted to do. But when university was over and it was time to find a job, would we lose our identity, as a stream flows into a river? Would we be free in the age of technocracy? This question is at the heart of the philosophy of Herbert Marcuse, the inspiration behind the hippy movement and behind much of the student revolt of our time.

Marcuse says that in the highly industrialised capitalist societies freedom has been replaced by 'repressive tolerance'. Men are so enchained by the system of satisfying consumer demand that they are in fact prisoners. They can think of no alternative way of life other than working like bees for huge industrial firms in which they are little more than a number. Man has lost not only his individuality but his will to be an individual. This I understand to be Marcuse's message. The workers are still exploited but don't know that they are being exploited. People everywhere are unaware of their state. Choice is conditioned. Democratic institutions such as elections are part of the 'repressive tolerance'. The system can afford to be tolerant because it knows it has you safely chained to its needs.

The new tyranny is science which tries to lure all men into a state of bliss. According to Marcuse man has become one-dimensional and will only free himself through a political, economic and intellectual liberation. The political liberation implies a breakdown of all centralised forms of government and control. What will liberate one-dimensional man is the freedom from all economic forces which eventually implies the freedom from earning a living.

But this high-sounding political jargon speaks of an age far distant. Marcuse makes a direct appeal to the escapists, to hippies, to students and to 'drop-outs'. They are not yet part of the system, an enlightened minority. They alone can realise the true needs of the masses (who have been so completely indoctrinated that they now defend the system). Students, says Marcuse, are the only untainted adults. It is their duty to be violent, since no other means will show the totalitarian nature of the society. If they provoke the police and the police retaliate brutally, then the people can see that the police bulldogs are dictatorial bullies.

I think the picture is out of focus. My objection hinges on one point: what can society give? A purpose? Morality? God? My answer to these questions is ' No.' Society cannot give me the reason for living. It provides the setting in which I find myself able to do a number of things, and perhaps to discover a more profound point to life (although as Tolstoy shows in his novels, it is sometimes the people most tied to a job, like peasant farmers, who have understood more than anyone). If Marcuse is right, I, as a student, am not in the mainstream of society. I can look at it from a distance. What do I expect? Quite simply the maximum material comfort for everyone, for the sick, and the healthy. I'll take the burden of discovering the meaning to my life upon myself. Professor Ayer speaks of ' a demand for a set of values that will enable people to lead lives in which they can find more meaning'. But where do you find this meaning? In yourself. No one can put my soul into me. I must drag it up from the depths of my being. A job, the way you spend the time of day, can make it easier or more difficult but a job is not creative or destructive in itself. People assert themselves. Individuality emerges through any system, at any time. It is not the system that limits people but people who limit themselves. And most people do and always have done.

Too little credit is given to the positive side of the material society. Certainly more people value material things today because more people can afford to buy them. But the point of science and technology is that it reduces the amount of drudgery in life. Choice and taste have a chance to expand, people can live in more agreeable surroundings. If I buy a purple trouser suit (which I have seen on television, or in a magazine, and for which I have been properly conditioned) it is not because

I cannot live either without the suit or without the colour. But clothes are a part of human expression, part of a civilisation, just as much as a house, or a painting or a book. It is to this end that technology is directed and standards are raised by competition and variety. To attain a degree of excellence in anything material is, in my opinion, in no way degrading. Morality was divorced itself from production in the late Middle Ages. It is the individual who must decide what is good for himself. It is up to each one of us to make science our servant not our master.

Are people and their personalities being 'bought off' by material things? I don't think so. I shall not devote my life solely to earning money. I shall write because it is my deepest desire. How I am judged by other people will, I hope, not deter me from writing. It is my means of expression, and I feel I have something to express. I am not aware of any economic infringement of my creative instincts, though admittedly I am still a student. However, if I do lose my determination, what fault can it be other than the weakness of my own character? Richard is certain that he wants to be a film director, and he is prepared to do any amount of work, for however little money, to arrive at the point where he can express himself freely in films. Ned is writing a novel. We are in a creative atmosphere, a university, and each of us wants to make an individual contribution. Some of us will, some will only dream of doing so.

Science has given us radio and television, the greatest of mass media. Television can indoctrinate us with advertisements and it can encourage us to buy what we might not want. (Here it is up to everyone to exert judgement and not merely absorb things like a sponge.) But, far more important, television has vastly facilitated the spread of knowledge. It has increased people's awareness of the conditions of other men. It provokes thought. It is a mass medium that can deal in the abstract by transmitting ideas through pictures or discussion. It brings the creative lives of other people into all types of homes. Not so much in France perhaps where, to the shame of the country, the television is firmly in the hands of de Gaulle.

Through television the new left wing movement among the young – which had its most dramatic climax in the French 'revolution' of 1968 – was given world wide publicity.

The new left sees the challenge to the societies of Western Europe centred in the universities. These will become the critical fulcrum of society. The thought was at first exciting. It needed much consideration. The young people themselves who led the movement would bear the burden of their own philosophy.

To start the fire of any revolt a spark has to fall on a material grievance on which all students will take a stand. On the Continent the grievances are abundant: acute overcrowding, boring curricula, minimal student representation, and above all, total neglect by the staff. In Italy several communist-inspired riots protesting against conditions found sympathetic support among the majority of students. The attitude of the professors remained negative and by the New Year an explosion was overdue. As always, the Italian Communist Party was the first to seize on the potential revolutionary situation, this time with a purpose: the elections were only a few months away. It was above all the communist students who roused their fellows, hoping to provoke the police into repressive action that would turn the people against the Government.

Throughout the autumn of 1967 there had been great unrest in Germany. In early June a young man, Benno Ohnesorg, had been shot during a demonstration against the State visit of the Shah of Persia. Rioting in the streets had followed. From Martin Baehr, the brother of Ulrich, I had received a long account of the battles. The police had shown appalling violence, punching and hitting everyone within sight, until one had finally shot a student. Martin concluded his long letter with the remark, 'Students in Germany were met by opposition from all sides, which was the best guarantee of their solidarity.' The police showed great brutality; the Springer Press launched its attacks day after day, in crude, emotive language; the Government suspended the university constitution and eventually forbade all political assemblies in the city of West Berlin. The revolutionaries, with their Che Guevara-cum-Red Guard tactics, disrupted the FU in the winter term with 'go-ins', which involved the highly democratic process of breaking up a lecture by shouting. The professors retaliated and suspended their lectures. The New Year came in on a wave of riots in Rome, followed by an occupation of the University, Italian action which encouraged the Berlin students at the FU and the *Technische Hochschule*. The professors were in no mood to discuss the proposed reforms. Nothing stimulates revolt so much as blank opposition.

At Christmas the Horror Commune (the same *Kommune* that I had visited), with their inimitable humour, left leaflets all over the Kaiser Wilhelm Gedächtnis Kirche, scoffing at the West Berliners for being conservative and *bourgeois*, for having created a cult against the left. 'We will crucify you,' the letter exclaimed, ' we will cut off your ears and roast you.'

The reaction of the Press, particularly of the Springer Press was interesting. *Die Welt* writes, ' It is a depressing fact that Ulbricht has in our own university, the Free University, that following which he has been unable to obtain in his own country.' In the more popular Press articles read, ' Communists need only wait for the *Bundesrepublik* to fall into their hands unless the people assert themselves.' The *Heimkehrer* ran impassioned articles on the appalling bad taste of the event. 'How would Christ have handled this?' it asked, and answered, 'He would have said, " My father's house is a place of worship for all people. You have turned it into a political arena."

Police brutality and the persistence of the Springer Press recording in blatantly melodramatic language all student activity, united moderates and extremists, and throughout the winter the protest movement grew. From the letters of friends I could see the different trends. Götz enunciated the principal points of university reform that all students hoped for: intermediary examinations, a course of more general studies before studying a specialised subject, a reduction in the number of years necessary to qualify as a teacher (as yet, including time spent as a junior teacher, fixed at ten years).

Martin was enraged by police brutality and by the fallacious reports of the Springer Press, designed to arouse the strong anti-communist bias of West Berliners, not only against the idiotic militants, but against students in general. This was not difficult. In West Berlin, as I had seen for myself, anti-communist feeling was vehement and the new philosophy, although not affiliated to an existing system, was in spirit a Marxist movement.

In the winter term of 1967 Rudi Dutschke exhorted his fellow students to follow the new wave of thinking. His teacher was Marcuse: a convenient and highly adaptable thinker. In open debates, articles and interviews Dutschke laid down the essence of the student revolt. It had two sides, national and international. In the German context there was an acute need for less overcrowded university conditions, for more professors. Germany needed an opposition to the government – the Grand Coalition between the Christian Democrats and Socialists was sapping the strength of all progressive thought for the political well-being of students, and indeed citizens. Dutschke criticised strongly the absence of opposition in parliament and the lack of contact between the German electorate and the government. To Dutschke, the reason for unrest, apart from the amorphous political situation, was the economic miracle and the pressure that the expanding economy was bringing on all students. They were part of the system of production, exploited by the German capitalists to further the economic state. Authoritarianism was on the increase with the end of the economic miracle. The Government had established a process of ' de-politicising ' the people, which explained the lack of interest in politics. All those involved in the economic system were being brainwashed. Here Dutschke launched into the theories of Marcuse on the ' conditioning of man by science '. ' It is deeply disturbing and sad that in " free " Germany, once again a man can be killed for his political beliefs.'

In February, the extremists led protest movements which expanded into wide-scale rioting that caused the Government to intervene and to ban all political assemblies. The interesting aspect of the revolt was the attitude of the citizens. They staged counter-student marches, wrote inflammatory letters to the newspapers, ' the students are trying to undo all that we have built up in twenty years of hard work.' The ordinary citizen, with an inherent hatred of anything that smacks of socialism or communism, rose in fury against the students. The Springer Press was only a reflection of what many people felt and said, but it did its best to exhort to violence.

' Communists are among us,' ran the *Berliner Morgenpost*, ' but Berliners will stand together as they always have in days of old' (1 March). Counter-revolutionary slogans, *lieber tot als rot*, (rather dead than red) were recorded in all newspapers.

Throughout February the more objective newspaper, *Die Zeit*, was reporting the violence of opposition to students. On 9 February it ran a leader, 'Civil War in Berlin?' Letters from German friends confirmed the danger of civil war. 'Anti-communism here is a disease,' Götz wrote, 'the inhabitants of this city live on a knife edge. They demand their security; they abhor the use of terror. Fear is the main counter-revolutionary force.' To Götz this was understandable. The older generation of West Germans had suffered immensely in times of terror and anarchy; with their vivid memories of the recent past, coupled with the fear of 'left wing' movements, it was hardly surprising that they should turn against the rioters. What saddened Götz was the viciousness of their behaviour. In fights at the end of February between students and West Berliners, newspapers reported that the mob had gone mad. Citizens were screaming to kill the students, to 'lynch them to the nearest tree'.

Student efforts to enlighten the majority were not succeeding. Eghart commented sadly on the spring of revolution. 'Every movement in this country is one of extremism. As the movement to the left increases among the young, so the people veer further to the right. Kiesinger spoke of the danger from the right. Danny Cohn-Bendit, at his recent trial in Frankfurt, repeated the same warning. Nothing worries the Germans so much as the increasing support for the NPD, the neo-Nazi party. But it was on the left that the German public vented its anger. The left implied rioting and anarchy and high-flown talk about discovering the needs of West Germans. It was in a climate of vehement public hostility that Dutschke was shot in April 1968. With the loss of its most influential leader and speaker, with the severe repression of riots, the student movement seemed temporarily defeated by the German public who voiced a massive 'no' to the 'enlightened' minority.

But revolution was carried on the wings of television as it had been from its beginning. From China came the Red Guards and the early ideas of cultural revolution. Naturally these ideas needed some modification. Western Europe would not be likely to accept the word of Chairman Mao as the only book of any interest. Nor would it be likely to ban chess as an imperialist and revisionist game—the Russians always win—nor proclaim ping-pong as the truly democratic sport—guess who wins at that. Nor would it be likely to change the sequence of its traffic lights so that red, instead of signifying stop, meant go, go man go with the Red Revolution. Television had transmitted the scenes of the Red Guards in charge of China, proclaiming Mao and their new ideals in the streets. Moral solidarity is very alluring. Ideas of revolution and social transformation spread to America, to Columbia and Berkeley, which is in the radius of Marcuse's immediate influence (he teaches at Santa Barbara). From America it crossed the Atlantic to Europe. In England the movement was in embryo; in Italy the riots raged; Germany followed suit and now it was, to my astonishment, *l'heure de la France.*

10

Paris
May 1968

'*A Paris les étudiants s'amusent,*' thus began a letter from Dominique Rossignol, dated early in May. News of the violent student riots in Paris had been flashed across the television screens of the world. All the faculties were occupied by students. In Saint Germain and the Latin Quarter barricades had been erected across the streets, students had taken their stand and fought, and often won, fierce battles with the police who had used tear gas and, many people alleged, acid bombs. Hugues produced reports, written at ten in the morning, after spending the night in the streets fighting. He told of the increasing confusion, 'what I had understood on Monday with great difficulty was no longer true on Tuesday, and on Wednesday the problem was totally different so that I was no longer sure whether there was in fact anything constructive to understand.'

On 16 May a letter from Dominique read, 'Last night the violence was indescribable. Police received an order to disperse all students. They set fire to the barricades, the air was full of tear gas; the Government might fall. . . .' I spoke to Dominique on the telephone. She urged me strongly to come if I could, and not to delay. The next morning I was on an eight o'clock aeroplane.

I shall never forget Paris Occupied. There was a joyous anarchy in the air, inescapable and contagious. Excitement shone in the eyes of those nameless, faceless students who had filled the lecture halls, in former days, subdued and silent. The Boulevard Saint Germain near the Drugstore, the Deux Magots, the Latin Quarter were alive with young people, running, shouting and happy. In the bright morning sunshine I found myself outside the Faculty of Medicine. Red banners hung above the entrance. At first I thought it might be some celebration and then I remembered the whole of the University of Paris was in the hands of the students. Student power was splashed on the grey walls. 'Everyone is free to enter' was painted on a flag. A crowd of students were pushing their way either in or out of the portico, taking leaflets that were being handed to them giving the latest details of the fight against the Government.

In the café exactly opposite the Faculty I sat down and drank a cup of coffee and watched. Some students wearing black armbands were directing the early morning traffic. I turned to a boy sitting at the same table as myself and asked him who they were. '*Service d'ordre,*' he explained. It was the student police force established by the *Union Nationale d'Etudiants Français* (UNEF), a weak, indecisive organisation that was trying to keep hold of the anarchic situation. 'What do you want in your Faculty?' I asked this friendly person who was in his third year of medicine, 'We want reforms and a greater degree of participation; we want to be able to change things without coming up against a Ministry of Education that takes a year to get us a new piece of chalk.'

He adumbrated the development of the movement. The revolt had begun at Nanterre, the new Faculty of Letters. On 22 March a committee met in an amphitheatre at Nanterre, protesting against the arrest of six members of the National Committee of Vietnam. The room was occupied. This was the first stage of the movement of the 22 March. Since January the revolutionary philosophy had been gaining momentum. Danny Cohn-Bendit, a student of sociology at Nanterre, and his friends wanted to replace the traditional university by the critical university. Cohn-Bendit refuted all existing student organisations. His aim was (and no doubt still is) to make of each university an autonomous institution, 'directly democratic', and free from all economic pressure. It must at all costs be kept out of the social system or it will lose its independent critical nature. To be the tortured conscience of the nation is the future designated for universities.

And it is only possible to awaken a nation through 'extra-parliamentary opposition', active protest outside the confines of parliamentary democracy (which has ceased to be a democracy).

Since January the Faculty had been thrown into disorder. A friend, Catherine Courroux, a student of Latin at Nanterre, an attractive and very positive girl, described the spring term: 'Since January the Faculty has been in chaos. The left were constantly interrupting lectures. Sometimes they literally threw the professor out of the hall.' The revolutionaries were 'sociologists, residents of those gloomy halls, jealous of the rich day students'. Catherine was not unbiased; she hated violence. In early May a sort of gang warfare broke out between the extreme left and the extreme right. 'Mobs of rampaging students ran through the buildings,' Catherine remembered, 'armed with dustbin lids and crash helmets.'

As a result Nanterre was closed by the Rector. Cohn-Bendit and his associates marched to the Sorbonne to try and arouse his student friends. The pattern was the same as in Nanterre: students occupied the Sorbonne. Then the Rector, Roche, made a fatal error. He lost his head and on 2 May ordered the police to move into the Sorbonne to clear the students and close the university. Police had not entered the courtyard of the Sorbonne since the Middle Ages. 'They entered the university,' Dominique told me indignantly. 'It is a sanctuary. We have nothing, no individuality, no personality, but we do have the university. It's all that is ours.' The reaction of students of all degrees against the intervention of the police was the same: ' la solidarité contre le pouvoir '. It is possible that nothing would have happened if the police had not moved into the Sorbonne. On 13 May the Sorbonne was re-opened and re-occupied.

The brutality of the police had shocked not only students but also Parisians. 'No code of law was observed,' Dominique told me. 'Police broke into houses and searched flats with no warrants or authority. If they found students hiding they beat them up. In the streets if they saw a group of young people they set upon them. It was not safe for anyone to walk in the Quartier Latin in daylight. The CRS attacked any pedestrian, foreigner, young girl or boy, who might have been a student.' The whole population of Paris had been profoundly disgusted by the behaviour of the CRS, who no doubt thought they were back in Algeria fighting a full scale war.

My new friend offered to take me on a tour of the occupied

Faculty of Medicine. We left a café packed with students talking excitedly around the small tables, crossed the street and pushed our way through the crowded entrance. It might have been Victoria Station in the rush hour. Loudspeakers blared out official-sounding messages; several hundred students wandered through the halls or stood on the stone staircases talking. A notice board with a plan of the activities of the building was the centre of much attention. A system of study groups to compile university reform had been under way for the last week. I was struck by the efficiency of the organisation in spite of the noise and apparent confusion.

My guide explained what was happening: direct democracy had been brought to the Faculty. Students had formed, and were continually forming, work groups or commissions. Each commission, attended by several professors—for the teaching staff of the University was with the students in the reform movement – took a vote on all proposed issues. Then at the end of the day all the resolutions of the different commissions were submitted to a wider assembly that took another vote. All resolutions passed went to the *comité d'action*, a liaison committee, and from the *comité d'action* to the general assembly of all students of the Faculty. Once passed by the general assembly they were submitted to the *Doyen* of the Faculty as part of the whole programme of reform. The future of the University of Paris was in the hands of students and professors alike who had been given *carte blanche*.

We wandered through laboratories where tired bodies lay stretched out on dissecting tables (they had been sleeping there for days, my guide told me). In every classroom discussion groups between young teachers and students were in progress. The passionate enthusiasm of the students, moderate in their political opinions, was startling. 'At last we have the feeling that we are doing something,' my guide explained, 'and the professors and teachers, particularly the younger ones, are as delighted as we are that at last we can reform the system.'

Placards advocating autonomy for the University were splashed throughout the building. Pamphlets issued by the *comité d'action* spoke of a plan sanctioned by professors to give students the power of veto over all essential questions of the University. 'What does this mean?' I asked. Were they to have control over the money, over the election of the professors? My guide was surprisingly realistic. 'We are asking for a yard to get an inch. We will not obtain autonomy, but the end result will be a much greater degree of control over internal affairs, over the curriculum, the conditions, over the distribution of money. Most professors would like this. They have been hampered by the centralised organisation of the system.'

Medical students seemed older than the average French students. Their course lasts anything up to eight years and in this time of crisis they seemed among the most serious and constructive people. They had been the first to set up commissions and to tackle in earnest the reform of their syllabus which was generally considered out of date in the modern era of medicine. The atmosphere at the Faculty of Medicine was anti-revolutionary. My guide explained, 'If you study medicine it is because you want to be a doctor. We do not have the same problems as sociologists who don't know what to do once their degree is over. We are not concerned with reforming the world but with reforming our syllabus and the organisation of our University.'

Two hundred students had been sleeping in the improvised dormitories on the top floor. I was surprised that so many students were conspicuously well dressed. Girls in the latest *minipulls* and bell-bottomed trousers passed through the hall. The French chic never dies, not even in time of revolution. The faculty library had been turned into a Press office and reception centre for journalists. The Press attaché tried to explain the international and political significance of the reform. He was a member of the *comité d'action*, briefed by his seniors on the official handout. He was, however, a novice. 'It's all in this book,' he muttered and fumbled through a manuscript of several pages. 'The aims of the revolt,' he read out loud, and turning to me asked, 'Would you like to take it down?' I shook my head.

I left the Faculty of Medicine for Dominique's house where I found her about to go to the Sorbonne. She was in high spirits. Dressed in anarchic black, with her straight blonde hair falling down to her waist, I had never seen her look so happy.' *C'est merveilleux ce qui se passe.*' She spoke in the plural, '*nous*'. 'Now it's up to us to reform the University. We must have free political expression, a new curriculum.' We walked along streets still littered with rubble and overturned dustbins. Near the Sorbonne, along the Boulevard Saint Michel the roads were crowded; no police were in sight. Members of the *service d'ordre* were directing traffic.

Dominique was about to join a commission to discuss a new curriculum for the history degree. 'For one year I have been just a name and a number. Now, quite suddenly, I have an identity. I am free to be heard.' We came into the Place de la Sorbonne. The cafés were crowded. ' No *flics* [policemen] anywhere you see,' Dominique went on. '*On fait ce qu'on veut, quoi.* You can dance and sing.' In the courtyard of the Sorbonne, advertised for that evening, were folk-song guitar recitals and plays by the Théâtre de la Sorbonne. '*Pas de joie, pas de révolution,*' Dominique explained. Cloth slogans hung from first-floor windows: 'freedom to the masses', 'solidarity with the workers'. Red paint smeared the walls, a loudspeaker rose above the noise to announce the latest decision of the strike committee, or the action committee. Everyone was ' *camarade* ', friends and strangers. Faces peered out from windows on all floors, staring down at the shifting crowd.

Nodding to passing 'comrades' Dominique led the way through the courtyard into the corridors and lecture halls. Students were everywhere, talking, standing, rushing up stairs. Signs in red paint splashed across the dirty white walls read ' let's be cruel,' ' down with Gaullist absolutism.' A notice pointed to an improvised Kindergarten for the children of workers, ' They think of everything,' Dominique laughed. We came into a large hall. Canteen was dishing out coffee and sandwiches free. ' Several hundred students sleep here every night. They have to live,' Dominique explained. At the entrances to the Sorbonne I noticed students holding out hats, '*pour nos camarades.*'

Modern art, sculpture, paper designs and paintings stood prominently in the halls and passages. ' It was only classical art before,' Dominique explained. ' The feeling is of the moment. We want to live in the immediate present.' On bill-boards and doors pictures of police brutality were prominently displayed beside red painted slogans,

L'imagination prend le pouvoir
It is forbidden to forbid. Law of 13 May.

'My mind feels free, for the first time,' Dominique told me, yet she was not strictly a revolutionary. She did not believe that students would bring about a social revolution, but passionately hoped for educational reform, and for a better deal for students after they had finished their studies, 'So we can end the rat race of getting five and six degrees before you can find a job.' However, when I spoke to officials of the committees, and to any student who would spare two minutes, I realised that in the Sorbonne the educational reform had become of less interest. '*Le mouvement s'est politisé.*' 'Now we must overthrow the Government,' the secretary of one of the committees told me emphatically. 'De Gaulle is a fascist; he censors the Press; the radio and television are his puppets. And he still tries to persuade us we live in a democracy.' 'Under five per cent of workers' children are at university.' 'We have got to overthrow the social order. Destroy the "bourgeoisie consommatrice".'

And what would follow? It was of course a difficult question. 'Smaller units,' said a member of the action committee, 'Participation for everyone.' 'And what if people hand over their share of "participation", so that once again management is in the hands of a few?' I asked. 'They won't,' he exclaimed, 'people will feel differently.' I was doubtful. In Yugoslavia, the workers' committees that run the factories are under heavy criticism from the students (who run against the stream of liberalisation in Eastern Europe and who, strangely enough, hanker after a more rigid form of communist party control). Students accuse workers of betraying communism because the workers are developing a management side to industry which makes the company more efficient. They are choosing profit and not participation. But at the Sorbonne the optimistic spirit of revolution was strong. 'This is a national movement,' said a short, black haired young man with pride. He wore a red armband, so I knew he must be some sort of official. 'We want to be united in spirit,' he said emphatically, 'that is except for the capitalist exploiters. For them we can have no sympathy.'

I left the Sorbonne for Hugues's flat. He looked tired, and to my delight his face was scratched from fighting on the barricades. 'While we fought we were united emotionally, everyone was incensed by police brutality,' he told me. 'The militant left saw their chance and are trying to make a political revolt.

The workers, too, saw a chance to take advantage of the " revolutionary" situation, and have joined with the left. Workers and
students have joined, not out of mutual love, but because they
feel that it is the way to get their demands.' Hugues doubted that
the two groups had much in common. The danger, he felt,
was that the students were being exploited by political parties;
that unless they tried to regain the lead from the extreme left,
they might lose everything. ' Cohn-Bendit and the committee of
the 22nd March want a total revolution.' He had spoken to
several members of the committee. First they asked him if he
knew how to make a molotov cocktail (no one else did). Then
they told him that they were going to take over the Press and
television. Hugues asked what plans they had for using the mass
media to their own ends. ' Use it? – we don't want to use it. Just
destroy it,' was the answer.

Not all students were extremists. In fact the majority I spoke
to were not. In their hands, and in the hands of the teachers and
professors (almost all in favour of a radical change in the educational system) was the reform programme.

I combed the Faculty of Law, Sancerre, the annexe of the
Faculty of Letters, and Sciences Po, where I was given a profit-
able tour by a humorous revolutionary, who didn't believe for a
moment that the Government would fall. '*Le Grand Charles*
won't throw in his hand without a fight,' he told me, but hoped
for a better university system. Sciences Po and the Faculty of Law
had a much more respectable atmosphere than the Sorbonne.
There was less of Che Guevara and Mao, more serious discussion on a complete revision of the curriculum, the examination
system and the internal structure of the university. I looked
around for Alain, and was not surprised to search in vain. I was
enchanted to find so many young French turned anti-Gaullist,
and very impressed by the co-operation of students and teachers,
by the industry and seriousness with which they took on the
huge task of educational reform. The Sorbonne was held in
slight scorn. '*Ils ne sont pas sérieux.* All they do is listen to
pop music.' Leaflets, in small print, were handed out at the
entrance of the litter-covered floor by serious individuals. They
were written in accordance with such a stringently logical plan
that the life had been drained from the words. ' We must overthrow the consumer society,' followed by *petit* (*a*) *petit* (*b*) and

ten sub-divisions. 'They are so indoctrinated that they can't even emerge from their ludicrous filed and catalogued train of thought. At Sciences Po and the Polytechnic, it's all the same. They are robots. . . .'

I left the industrious atmosphere of Sciences Po to enter the equally industrious Faculty of Law and hear an assembly meeting. 'My own Faculty was one of the last to join the movement,' Hugues told me as we made our way to the amphitheatre. He added, 'The most serious discussions were being held not here but among the fourth-year students in the old Faculty.' The general assembly had been called for five o'clock and by the time we arrived it had begun. It was a chaotic meeting. Over a thousand students had crammed into the hall, but hardly a resolution was heard above the noise and jeers of a crazy group at the back.

After the meeting adjourned and the students flooded out of the exit doors, the dedicated discussion groups formed once again in the huge amphitheatre. Dotted among the empty rows of benches, students and teachers talked in low voices, discussing every minute aspect of the specific topic they had chosen. As one student told me, 'For the first time there is a chance to get to know the teachers, and those professors who take an interest. The university really is a close-knit body.' The discussion groups sat from early morning until late at night. Anyone was free to join, to listen in, or to form one of his own. The creative revolution, a complete transformation of French universities, was in the hands of the moderate students and their teachers who wanted to channel revolution into evolution.

However, for the moment Paris was in the hands of the extremists. Standing outside Sciences Politiques, I watched a battle between a group of *occident* (right) and the *gauche* (left). A group of *occident* students and teddy boys wearing crash helmets and carrying heavy sticks and dustbin lids attacked the two hundred or so students standing outside Sciences Politiques listening to a broadcast on the loudspeaker. Suddenly stones and several chairs were hurled into the air. The right wing group was deterred by the numbers of Sciences Po students, and shouting, swearing, and threatening the small group of spectators, they marched across the Boulevard Saint Germain in the direction of the Odéon, the theatre that had been occupied for several days.

I saw the Odéon on the evening of Dominique's twentieth birthday. Typically, she did not mention it until the evening. With Hugues we went out to celebrate. I doubt if ever again she will remember a birthday held in such a spirit of revolution. The rain was falling hard and in a crowded café in the Place de la Sorbonne she, Hugues and I sat and ate ice creams. The noise around us was deafening. Over each table students and young people were deep in earnest conversation. The rain as it beat on the windows made the atmosphere even more intense.

A young girl came up to Dominique. She was organising the Cultural Revolution in the Faculty of Letters. She was attractive, intelligent and excited. ' Perhaps we will have a chance to make a world in our image; not like us of course, but with rejuvenated ideals.' A man soaked to the skin wearing black leather pushed past; the conversation was interrupted. Cups of coffee floated past on a tray. ' *Garçon,*' shouted a voice and then corrected itself, ' *Camarade*'. The girl went on, 'There will be a rejuvenation, in television, in the theatre.' She spoke in vague terms of a renaissance of arts, of teaching all people to appreciate the arts, of giving painting, music and literature a place of pre-eminence in the New World.

' You know the television has been censored,' she said to me. ' We have been stifled by this whole régime, and now it looks as if it might be over. I feel I can breathe again.' She was called away. Another tray of coffee passed by. The rain slashed and cracked on the glass; a jazz blues wound itself round the low hum of conversation that rose and fell like waves on a beach. 'It's so strange,' Dominique pondered, as she ate an enormous ice cream, 'but people whom you have known for a long time, and who used to seem as dull as everyone else, have suddenly come to life. They speak, they have feelings, take a part. *C'est merveilleux.*'

We left the Odéon. The entry was barred by officials. Dominique dismissed this unnecessary bureaucracy. I heard her say in positive, articulate French something about the *Daily Mail* (I had been given a retainer by the said newspaper a few months before). Within a minute I was handed a scrap of paper with the word 'Press' scribbled on it, signed by at least four people, and we were inside the theatre. We climbed up red carpeted steps littered with paper, stepping over sleeping bodies. We pushed open a door and sat inside an empty box. The stage was fully lit. In the stalls groups of students were sleeping, or talking. A spindly man was singing a song about the joys of love making, the American pigs in Vietnam, the blood sucking capitalists, and let's lynch de Gaulle. On the ground beside us a boy sat picking his feet. 'The culture [sic] in this country stinks. It's capitalist orientated. Men must be released. We must suffocate the *bourgeoisie* so the workers of France can breathe. Direct democracy,' he muttered. 'Does that mean the *bourgeois* will have a say?' I asked nervously. 'The *bourgeois* deserves nothing, and he shall get nothing.' We left the box, and walked through the corridors, past unshaven, tired students into the cool, refreshing air.

For several days I felt anarchistic. I rode Dominique's bicycle on the left hand side, I ignored most traffic lights, called out '*camarade*'. The freedom sucked in everyone, French students and foreigners. That is, almost everyone. I had an appointment to meet Dominique in a café on the Boulevard Saint Michel. I walked into the café, sat down and called a waiter. '*Camarade*,' I began. He lashed out with a stream of invective and ordered me out. I had got the wrong café. This was a right-wing stronghold.

The Sorbonne remained the centre of the 'revolution' throughout. Each evening meetings were held in its amphitheatre. I went to many, but one evening in particular I shall never forget. This big intellectual evening in the grand amphitheatre had been well advertised. By the time that Hugues and I arrived crowds of people, mostly students, were clamouring at the inner gates of the Sorbonne that give access to the Grand Amphitheatre. 'It's full to the ceiling,' a bearded hippy shouted out. 'The discussion will be relayed in the courtyard. Go outside.' What an idiotic suggestion! To hear Sartre's voice in the courtyard was not at all the same thing as to hear and see him speak and to watch the reaction of the audience.

I pushed forward and produced the improvised press card that I had been given at the Odéon. '*Daily Mail*, London, *Londres, je viens de Londres*,' I shouted above the din. The hippy looked at me. He was not more than twenty, probably the same age as me; it was a battle of wills among people of the same generation, '*pour la presse. . . .*' I garbled some explanation in French, fast and fluently. He muttered, and then pulled the door back quickly. ' *Vite.*' I squeezed through, Hugues stood on the other side, a little perplexed. ' *O mon Dieu,*' I thought. 'He's with me,' I explained in French. 'I can't possibly go without him.' The hippy was very suspicious. 'What is he?' I gave a positive answer, 'My interpreter. . . .' Before the hippy had time to think Hugues had squeezed through the door and we were racing up the wide stone stairs. I heard another ' official' who had been watching, say to the bewildered hippy, ' What exactly does he interpret?'

But it was too late. We were on the third floor of the Sorbonne, jammed into the corner of an upper balcony. Through the crack between a shoulder and a head I could see the stage. Sartre was sitting between the student leaders Geismar and Sauvageot of the UNEF. He was not speaking; the hall echoed with the voice of a well-known journalist who was answering questions. I struggled forward to get a better view of the lecture hall. The air was unhealthy and sticky; smoke curled up towards the lights. Students jostled and packed into every square inch of the hall; rows of faces filled the highest balconies and the gangways. The amphitheatre, like an opera house on its opening night, was bulging to the rafters. Bodies hung like washing over the balconies, and the most adventurous men had even scaled the walls and railings to get a seat, either in the lap of a huge statue of Victor Hugo or Pascal, or to sit in the arms of Richelieu or another of the statues fixed to the lower balcony with a view over the stalls on to the stage. The three thousand or more people, breathing and exuding the thick white air, swayed and moaned restlessly. Nurses with Red Cross caps on their heads clambered over the crouching or half standing bodies to reach fainting students. Throughout the evening I saw the nurses pushing their way through the dense crowd with mugs of water.

Once my eyes were used to the scalding air, and my lungs had filled with the suffocating carbon dioxide, I devoted all my attention to the stage. Sartre got up to speak. A roar of applause rose in the huge hall. Television cameras and photographers moved in. Shouts of disapproval raged around the terrified camera men who quickly turned off their powered lights. 'Now the film star takes over,' Hugues whispered scornfully. ' I come to you' Sartre announced calmly and confidently through the microphone, 'not as a politician but as an intellectual.' I could see that he was going to try and explain what exactly the revolution was about. A difficult task.

He lasted forty minutes. Rowdy shouts and the continual noise made any discussion impossible. Questions could not be heard, abuse drowned much of what he said, abuse from a vociferous minority, drunk with alcohol or perhaps tiredness, who shouted at everything and anything said that evening. Sartre tried to discuss, 'the movement must be unanimous . . . you must have a programme. . . .' Former members of the *Front Populaire* aired their views. 'We failed . . . it's up to you to succeed. . . .' Sartre sat quietly and patiently, trying to hear the questions that were shouted at him, but seemed to get tangled up in the smoke, and reached him only in a garbled, incomprehensible form. A woman factory worker, near the front, was determined to be heard. 'What are they going to do for us?' she shouted. 'All these students, are they in revolt for themselves or for all of us?'

Sartre tried to reassure her on the bona fide international intentions of the revolt. 'But do we want the same things?' she kept asking. 'Education is all very well, but we have to earn money to feed ourselves.' This was getting interesting. The conversation was interrupted by some character who wanted to ask a question on Sartre's novel, *La Nausée*. Boos and hisses forced the young man to sit down, 'This is not a literary session but an effort to clarify the importance of what you are doing,' came the writer's pompous reproof. But Sartre was little help; he produced stock Marxist jargon (which was warmly received) and said repeatedly that a transformation of society was in the offing . . . '*Maintenant ça suffit,*' he said quite suddenly and left.

The hall spilled half its contents into the corridors and into the cool air of the courtyard. Hugues and I moved down into the stalls. Several working men and women stayed behind. The back rows of the seats filled with bodies that stretched and lay still. A discussion resumed. This time it was the French factory workers, some from Renault, who set the pace. 'You students think you should run the world, when you haven't even had a job!' Another angry worker said, 'We don't want to have anything to do with you. You don't know what work is.'

'Revolution, for you *c'est la bagarre* [it's a brawl], for us it's several weeks with no wages, and a hungry family at home. . . .' 'All you think of is material wealth. You just want to become a *bourgeois* like the rest of this country. You aren't capable of a revolution . . .' an angry student screamed out. There was a moment of uneasy tension before a worker, obviously well in with the students, stood up and in a family doctor-cum-Harold Wilson way of speaking told the assembly that their struggle had the same objective : the downfall of the Government. 'Don't let's waste energy, we both want the same thing, down with de Gaulle.' On this safe note applause broke from the tired crowd. Everyone rose to sing the *Internationale*. I saw several people hesitate before standing, but they rose.

As we walked out of the hall, Hugues said, 'It can't last. The French workers are kindling this revolt only as long as it serves their ends, but they in no way support the social revolution. The worker is the backbone of the system and he believes that his best interests lie in the system.' We walked out into the courtyard; gratefully I breathed its cool air. By two o'clock most students and spectators had gone home except for the residents. I stood enchanted by the scene. Everything was still; the banners hardly moved in the night air, the stalls were deserted, the microphone silent. Lights from the courtyard windows streamed on to the stone floor, casting strange shadows. The high walls, long thin windows, the wooden doors, the porticos and statues and the baroque church rising against a sky bright with stars seemed a strange backcloth to revolution.

A group of workers and students were chanting the *Internationale* in one corner of the courtyard. Their voices were hardly heard against the pounding rhythm of a complete jazz band, including a grand piano, that was playing loudly on the platform in front of the church. We stood by the huge wooden church doors, watching and listening. Over a hundred students crowded round the pianist. The beat was compelling and couples jived on the church steps. On all floors the lights of the Sorbonne were blazing; they faded as they spread like a sheet over the large, still expanse of the courtyard, catching on the silver button of a coat, lighting a face or a smile. '*C'est la joyeuse anarchie,*' said a girl beside me, as she clapped to the music. 'And just think,' she went on, pointing to the rows of lights, 'all this is being paid for by *Papa l'État.*' In spite of the music, the Sorbonne seemed quiet. The violence and incoherence of politics had settled like dust in the corners of the courtyard, giving way to the gypsy gaiety of the revolt.

But with each day the gaiety was growing weaker. Even during the short time I was in Paris, the atmosphere changed. Something sad was in the air, as indefinable as the contagious revolt. Its high moral aims were reiterated at the Faculties of Law and Sancerre. Marcuse and Marx together enchained people in jargon, ' dictatorship of the proletariat ', ' direct democracy ', ' end to the consumer society ', there was a quick answer to everything. Opposition was discounted. The massacre of millions of Tibetans had worried no one; the only murderers in the world were Americans in Vietnam. Militant students claimed to be idealists, yet I could find no ideals that did not involve repression and cruelty. They had found an absolute and the fact that someone else might have settled for a different absolute was irrelevant. Direct democracy meant silencing everyone who disagreed, who would not kiss the ground before Saint Che, Saint Mao, Saint Castro and Lenin. I was sickened by the violence of language, the refusal to question the clichés which people mouthed like a religious chant, and most of all by the readiness to attack and destroy.

In other parts of the University of Paris more constructive and profound thinking was going on. The concept of the critical university was shared by many students. I quote from the journal, *Université Critique* : ' Universities should be structures of permanent disequilibrium.' ' To make a new society, and make the university its centre, this is the aim.' Professor de Jouvenel, who spent a great deal of time in the Faculty of Law, listening to his students, and often giving them encouragement and advice, came to England. He told me, ' Students don't want to become grocers and our society demands that everyone becomes a grocer.' In the arts faculties, always the most agitated, the future offered seems dull and humdrum after years spent contemplating great thoughts and great deeds. There should be some sort of job on a higher level that would satisfy the creative and intellectual faculties. For this, a transformation of society is needed. Professor de Jouvenel said, ' They want to reinstate the clerics of the Middle Ages, to have the job of teaching morals and conscience and "Higher Thoughts" to the population at large.'

In those discussions that I could follow I realised that the student revolt was in many ways a selfish revolt. People in their early twenties saw themselves as the guiding *élite*, with a taste for idealism that could not be satisfied behind a desk in a bank, or teaching at a blackboard. Egalitarianism was freely bandied about in the amphitheatres to tempt the visiting workers. But the militant students were suddenly silent when a car worker said that before starting a degree course every student should do two years' manual labour. I do not believe that any minority has the exclusive right to call itself enlightened, nor do I think that students are necessarily enlightened. Our approach is mostly spontaneous, the result of a book, a lecture, a television programme. Spontaneity is the cult of the age, in art, in the theatre and in music. University is one long spontaneous reaction to problems, political and personal. So what? The first impressions aren't always right. Why should they be? Why should people of fifty and sixty bow to the judgment of their children and their children's friends just because it's a new approach? Experience gives a wider basis of judgment. I'm not saying the oldest are the wisest, but I do believe that someone who has worked and supported himself has learnt something about life through his contact with other people.

I passionately supported the students in the demand for a new educational system, and in their determination to question accepted values and systems. But I was deeply saddened by the minority of militant students. I didn't find in them any intrinsic quality that would give them the right to become anyone's moral arbiter. Instead I found a confused feeling of being lost in a political system that didn't know what to do with its student population; a horror of a humdrum future; an impatient anger that people were not more high-minded than they appeared. Everywhere I found imagination stimulated by intolerance. There was an absence of any nobler human sentiment. No one set an example of self-denial; it was just talk.

London-Oxford

June – October 1968

'WILL it happen here?' was the nervous question being asked in England by worried parents, politicians, teachers, and of course the ever-topical BBC. To help the nation comprehend the rebellious youth of the world, the BBC had invited student leaders from Western and Eastern Europe, and one student from Columbia, to appear on a programme with Professor Robert Mackenzie. England awaited the programme with curious, rather fearful interest.

'Could such widespread revolt happen here?' was one of the questions we discussed at the Historical Society week-end in Cumberland Lodge, the London University retreat in Windsor Great Park. I got back from France just in time to drive to Windsor from London. Staying the week-end were about thirty students from King's, and four or five professors and teachers. The subject under discussion was the Second World War. The week-end was a continuous seminar. Some lectures were given by Professor Howard, who had resigned his post as head of our department to do research as a Fellow of All Souls at Oxford. Another lecturer was a fascinating professor from Jerusalem University. One teacher at a naval academy and one at an Air-Force school, both of whom had fought in the war, came to lecture. Throughout the week-end there was time to discuss the subject, to ask questions, to give any point of view. The Second World War was only one of the things we talked about. Major riots had flared up in Paris immediately after my departure. As students we wanted to talk about student violence and aims. Professor Howard, and members of staff in the History Department were also interested in the discussion which lasted late into the night.

When I thought that this sort of week-end, in which I really did have a chance to talk to professors and teachers, was part of my university life, I answered the question for myself, 'No, it wouldn't happen here.' Not only because we have none of the same grievances at university, but because most British institutions for all their faults are valued. They seem to perpetuate the freedoms that we care about the most. We have only voluntary censorship, in Press or television. Any political party is allowed, and any man can stand for election to Parliament. The legal system is less corrupt than most. There is a belief in British democracy and the values that it embodies, which is stronger among the young than any comparable belief in either France, Italy or Germany.

'Revolution in France – but then the French are always having revolution. They hate democracy, they like being ruled by some dictator to have the fun of overthrowing him.' These were the remarks I heard the following week-end when I went down to Oxford. Once again on Magdalen lawn, under the same hot sun, on the same green grass, I ate chicken legs and listened to the conversation. My brother and his friends admitted that they were delighted at the strike and the threat to de Gaulle. The story was being told with relish of the Labour MP Mr Shinwell asking in Parliament that the Government send a letter to France, saying that Britain would not think of joining the Common Market unless France put its internal affairs in order. (This was the phrase that de Gaulle had used in his last excuse for keeping Britain out of the Common Market.)

There were other things to think about. Andrew bought some bottles of beer, and with two other friends we clambered into a punt and headed down the river to where the boat races were being held. Andrew punted. He pushed the boat down-stream with a long pole, like a boatman on a gondola. Punts are comfortable but wet; still, I can think of no nicer way to spend a hot afternoon. Green banks, weeping willows and summer flowers bordered the river. As we floated past the Christchurch meadows I could see spires that pointed into the pale blue sky; people were strolling on the footpaths. The beer tasted cool and delicious, and only once did we scrape an oncoming boat – not our fault, Andrew claimed.

Finally we came in view of the crowds and the clattering punts, crammed together like a sea of floating shells. It was the last day of the rowing races, an event known as ' Eights Week ', an occasion in the Oxford summer term. Girls wore their craziest and brightest summer clothes. Bare midriffs were shaded by sombrero hats, and long dresses and Eliza Doolittle flowered hats were a contrast to shocking pink shorts and maternity mini-dresses. Boathouses, each belonging to a specific college, over-looked the river. From the roof tops and verandas of the boat-houses undergraduates, holding glasses and pieces of cake in their hands, looked down on the throng of moving people walking along the water's edge. There was talking and laughing, and a strange figure with a blazer, a boating hat and a cane, another with an enormous hat, and two bare legs that seemed (from above) to strike out of the hat itself.

Oxford boat races struck me as very odd; you didn't win if your boat was the first to cross the line, but only if you managed to bump the other boat on the way to the winning post. There was a lull in the noise, and laughter of over a thousand people as a race began. As it was, enthusiasts pushed to the edge of the water and to the front of verandas and roof tops, 'Come on Keble, move the boat, come on . . .' the boy in front of me screamed. Behind me I heard a girl's voice, 'How can I go out with James, without offending Terry, he's very sensitive you know.' A roar rose into the empty sky. The boy in front of me shouted and cheered; the girl behind me chatted on, 'When Terry found out he was simply furious. He's very melodramatic, but at the same time sensitive, most sensitive. . . .' Keble had won whatever major cup there was to win, and I felt for London. Three days later Oxford joined the bandwagon of student protest, the last of the universities to respond to the call of student power.

During the spring the flames of revolt had flickered through-out England : Essex, the Hornsey College of Art, East Anglia, London. At LSE a delegation of students went down to the docks to tell dockers that they were not the masters of their destinies. 'You don't know where you are going,' cried the students. 'Look, matey, just because *you* don't know where you are going (for all the education you're getting) doesn't mean that *I* don't know where I am going,' was the dialogue heard by one eye-witness.

In Oxford the newspaper *Cherwell* gave great prominence to the Storming of the Clarendon Building, on Monday, 3 June. The week before, the revolutionary committee of ninety put in an ultimatum demanding that the Proctors rescind their ban on the indiscriminate distribution of political leaflets. This was followed by a 'sit-in' in the Clarendon. After stormy scenes the Proctors gave way. *Cherwell* asked whether this had opened the flood-gates to student power. I spent the following week-end in Oxford and the answer was clearly, No.

The Press had devoted headlines and long articles to the Oxford revolt but, on closer questioning, the truth seemed far less glamorous than the Press made out. One friend who had watched the 'storming' of the Clarendon told me that most of the people who took part were from the Nuffield Research Centre, not undergraduates at all. The revolutionary committee of ninety is made up of many post-graduates and foreigners. But most startling of all was the general reaction. In Germany sit-ins were a matter of student interest for weeks. In Oxford when I asked people about what *Cherwell* called a 'Riot' many looked puzzled and said, 'Oh that . . . you call it a riot? Nervous post-graduates, with a guilt complex that they are not working yet . . .' was one caustic comment. Some people were openly against the riot and had paraded outside the Clarendon building with posters, 'We love the proctors.' My brother had passed the Clarendon Building to see what was happening. He disagreed with the 'sit-down' tactic. 'We've taken a vote,' one of the leaders screamed at him. 'We've taken a vote, we the committee of ninety, and this is our decision.' Andrew didn't feel that the committee of ninety or the Hart committee represented the majority of students. He was obstinate. 'Well, go and take another vote,' he answered.

I sat on the lawn at St Hilda's working. Nadine had booked a room for me in the main St Hilda's building in the guest wing. 'Feeling here is strong against militant protest. Oxford has a tradition of liberalism; it has never been an extremist university, and the militants never more than a tiny minority. And what's more,' she sighed, 'there's so much else to do. People are writing for university newspapers, they are acting plays or writing scripts, singing songs or playing violins, being intellectual or quite stupid, punting or hitting cricket balls. The greatest luxury of all is the time to think and talk and work.'

Michael Mire felt there were no grounds for revolution at Oxford. 'We have none of the grievances of French or German students, and then at Oxford the dons won't play ball. You need an opposition for a revolt, and the dons are mostly tolerant people, they don't provide the blank wall opposition that is so stimulating to revolt.' He told me of a protest he had made against the disgusting food of his college. 'I organised a group, and we arrived at the Dean's house and presented a petition. We had worked ourselves up into a militant state, and when the door opened, instead of sending us away he invited us in for a drink to discuss the matter and set up a sub-committee. It was totally disarming. . . .'

The leader in the *Cherwell*, following the student protest, was headed 'One battle won, but careful steps needed'. The Proctors had amended the Proctors' Memorandum, a statute defining their status as a body of authority. They had renounced their claim to be 'in loco parentis'. The leader gave its support to the non-violent Hart committee whose aim was 'a democratic community of scholars'. It continued, 'From now on we can rely on the constitutional methods the Hart Committee offers.' Many people I spoke to supported this leader. They were against violence. 'We don't need to resort to violence, whatever the committee of ninety says,' Nadine told me. 'Changes are made in Oxford through discussion.' The following week a joint Junior Common Room and Senior Common Room was set up in Somerville to discuss new ways of running the College.

But attention was diverted in Oxford, as in all universities, by the arrival of the leaders of the student revolt. The programme was recorded and then the student leaders agreed to stay on in London, at the LSE, to discuss revolutionary tactics for the future. The programme on television that had caused such a storm of attack from Conservative MPs, who announced that our liberties were at stake, was finally shown. The revolt of this year has been to a large extent created and nurtured by television; in England it was killed in one evening. There will no doubt be further demonstrations and protests, but the hope for any nationwide student revolt died when the European student leaders, and 'our' representative Tariq Ali, took part in an interview with Robert Mackenzie.

To the questions 'What are you against?' and 'What do you want?' the only clear answer was 'That is the wrong question.' Though it is not a stupid answer, it seemed so to millions watching television, who knew nothing of the New Left. Cohn-Bendit spoke of 'decentralisation', of a society without an *élite*, of a people's democracy not based on materialist values. A passionate anti-Establishment speech. When it came to the beautiful Yugoslav girl, she announced that in her country they wanted freedom of the Press, they wanted greater economic freedom (to buy the *bourgeois* goods), and they wanted more liberty to travel. Things were moving in that direction. . . . 'For us Tito is a hero.' At this point Cohn-Bendit could not conceal a grimace; soon after he was to insult the girl publicly and denounce her as a Tito stooge. The West German Marxist don proudly told everyone that many of his students were cleverer than he, and direct democracy was the ideal for the university. Again, the precise details were omitted. Who elects the professors? Who sets the examinations? Who chooses the courses? Who marks the examinations?

'They gave no answers,' a friend fumed the following day as we sat at King's discussing the programme. The inability on the part of all leaders to communicate their ideas was a bitter disappointment to my friends, who had listened with an open mind to what they hoped would be a profound and persuasive doctrine. To liberal minds, Danny had spoken words of tyranny when he said that it made no difference to him whether the French people voted for or against de Gaulle. People were part of a system, conditioned to respond. These were echoes of Paris, where support for de Gaulle, after his fighting speech denouncing anarchy and the danger of communism, was growing daily.

I was interested in the week-end of discussion on revolutionary tactics. From King's I crossed the stretch of road known as the Aldwych and walked a few steps up a side street to the main building of the LSE. The television cameras were out waiting for the filmstars: Danny the Red and Tariq Ali. Though advertised as a week-end debate on 'revolution', inside I could only find pre-conferences going on, where the filmstars were airing their views. Danny, his fat freckled face pink with indignation was shouting at a journalist for calling him 'Danny the Red'. 'Let's be polite,' he was shouting. 'Call me "Mister".' The Press left. Danny and his French colleague, Geismar, moved to another room. I stayed in the hall crammed with strange faces. The boy next to me came from the Hornsey College of Art. 'I would do away with all exams,' he told me. 'Not a bad idea,' I thought. Mine were to be in two weeks, if only it could be done quickly. . . . 'No,' he said (he was thinking aloud), 'No, we must have exams, but everyone must pass . . . that is true democracy?' 'Really? That suits me fine,' I said. 'You do all the work and I'll pass.' We were interrupted by the arrival of several student leaders; there was Geismar and an Italian, a German and a Japanese. Tariq Ali, who couldn't decide whether to sit or stand and shuffled at the back of the hall, made sure that he was not unnoticed.

The whole week-end at LSE was like a banger that fizzled out and failed to explode. In the hall, we listened to 'How to kill a Policeman' by the Japanese; to 'French Revolutionaries are the Greatest' by Geismar; to 'How to Murder White Men' by the Black Power representative; and to the only intelligent speech, by the Italian representative, who advised a straight-forward Marxist approach to revolution: fasten on a point of discontent, exploit it, and ensure that the discontent spreads until there is open war with the authorities and the government is overthrown. 'Extra-parliamentary opposition,' explained another spokesman, 'is the essence of revolt. Cause obstruction wherever you can. Bait the bulldog police, confront authority, it will crack . . .' 'And have a lot of fascists in charge, not bloody likely,' an art student beside me muttered while a deafening explosion of applause filled the hall.

I slipped out of the meeting, carrying leaflets from the radical student alliance, from the underground Press, from the revolutionary organisation Agit-Prop. The stairs were crowded with people still waiting to get into the halls. I could hear Danny Cohn-Bendit shouting. On the walls of the corridors were pinned sheets of the *International Times,* the foremost organ of the underground Press. Cartoon pictures filled the front page, 'Kill the bloody fuzz [police],' 'Steal whatever you can,' 'Free love', then a picture of love-making. All through the paper were bosoms and genitals, or articles from Black Power

Americans, 'We shall kill you, white man'. There were articles by students on the need for immediate anarchy, a sacking of shops, plunder of houses. On the back page an article entitled 'Half-fucked, half free . . .'

Outside in the street the air was calm. The jargon and the brutal violence of thought and language lingered. I felt sick and deeply saddened. I remembered a discussion I had had with a revolutionary friend at Cumberland Lodge. Direct democracy, he had explained, was the aim. Participation at all levels, in everything. 'And if I disagree?' 'We discuss and we vote.' 'And if I still disagree with the proposal, and carry the motion against?' 'We discuss, we persuade, you wouldn't disagree,' he added, 'it would be in the general interest. . . .' 'But if I did, if I persistently disagreed . . . ?' He shrugged his shoulders, and I lost my temper, 'I can tell you what you would do,' I exploded, 'you would kill me.' He had been so surprised by my vehemence, and so disturbed, because he was a charming friend, that we had quickly driven off to the pub and had a long pint of beer.

Danny the Red got a two-week extension of his forty-eight hour visa; the Yugoslav girl was rescued by the police from the 'coventry' imposed by the other revolutionary leaders. Then quite suddenly Danny the Red got bored and left. 'What a pity,' a friend of mine said. 'If he'd stayed longer he might have been made a life peer.'

Enough of revolution; it was time for examinations. I was faced with sessionals; three papers each three hours long. Richard and I tried to rouse support for a general boycott but of course no one joined. My own motives were not entirely honourable, I was nervous about passing and had good reason to be. Not that we think the written system bad. We don't. But we would like a combination of an essay written at leisure and a paper limited by time such as they have at Sussex and York, for example. At York your work throughout the year is also taken into account, and this reduces the strain. At Oxford, Finals are an appalling ordeal – forty hours of written papers in the space of a week.

I visited Oxford a few days before Finals, ostensibly to prepare for my own exams. Once again we were in Magdalen cloisters. Finals had begun a few days before. George and Conky Galitzine, both in the middle of their exams, sat drinking beer on the grass. A heatwave had settled in a week before arousing the usual interminable complaints. 'Isn't the weather terrible. So hot, you can't breathe. I have to stay indoors.' Anyone might have thought that the English sun was in the habit of giving daily matinées. Both George and Conky looked pale and tired; I concluded they had not seen daylight for days. Robin said, 'Only yesterday I met a boy who was trotting down the high street, starry eyed, shouting " I shall fail, I don't know anything, I can't face it." ' George added his own story. A friend of his had sat down to a history paper. A few minutes after the exam began, he had risen to his feet and shouted out, 'I can't do a bloody question,' and sat down as suddenly as he got up.

No one could deny that Finals are a great strain. Each year at Oxford there are some attempted suicides. 'Though in your last year, your tutor tries to do his best to see that you don't overwork,' Andrew told me. 'If you do crack up, before or during the exam, they will do what they can to help.' A friend of his had collapsed during Part Two of his finals in Greats. (In this four-year course Finals are divided into two parts. One section is taken after the first two years, another after the second two.) His tutors spoke up strongly on his behalf and the university awarded him an isocrat, the equivalent of a second though not in fact a degree. For a job though, an isocrat would be as good as a degree.

People run wild when Finals are over. I have seen this happen several times in Oxford. Third-year students sit their examinations in the Schools building. At twelve o'clock and five o'clock friends wait outside the entrance, to cheer those who have finished. It struck me as interesting that almost every undergraduate in any year knew the exact time-table of Finals. Nadine and I joined the crowd. Girls in bright summer clothes and large floppy hats waited by the railings. The first examinees emerged exhausted from the doors. Men wore gowns and women wore black hats with tassels, gowns and black stockings. People started to wave, to shout, to hug their friends. A bottle of champagne was produced, and drunk on the spot. The Proctor, who stood upright in his bowler hat, looked on severely. The year before champagne parties had been abolished. I could remember times when crates of champagne were carried to the gates, and froth and corks flew in the air to celebrate on the spot the end to the worst examination of a lifetime. Nadine saw a friend. He invited us to his champagne party on Trinity lawn where we spent the rest of the afternoon, drinking and eating and sharing in his euphoric jubilation.

Oxford was consumed by its summer life. There were nine college plays on that week, endless concerts, discussions and debates, and river parties, summer balls, and, the week after, several Commems. One rather special party was taking place that Saturday night. Randall, my younger brother, who had won an exhibition to Magdalen the year before and was going up in the autumn, was particularly anxious to go. The party was on a boat on the river. It was sponsored by the *Cherwell* in honour of the theatre critic Kenneth Tynan. Mr Tynan was a former Oxford undergraduate, and he was to be the subject of a BBC film, *Tynan's Oxford, Old and New*. The party chosen for television was an inauguration of the Oxford University Permissive Society. In its good *Daily Mirror* style the *Cherwell* had a piece advertising ' the famous televised party '.

' This party is reserved for the select few. Numerous lists have been drawn up; names chosen and rejected.

Only the cream of Oxford Society will be there to watch the cameras watch them mutually permitting.

The most stringent precautions will be taken to keep out unwanted guests and a cold muddy river awaits any strangers.

Andrew was going. ' Pity you can't come. Good for your book. You'll see all the Oxford trendies, the *Cherwell* wits all at their most self-conscious.'

My younger brother is an expert gate-crasher, I am an optimist and Nadine couldn't bear the thought of work so we had a democratic vote and invited ourselves to the party. Andrew led the illegal procession through the park to the St Catherine's barge on the river. Nadine and I had done our best to be permissive. She wore a shocking-pink trouser suit with bare arms and I, who had come unprepared, wore skimpy, virginal white. Andrew as always came out in the colours of the rainbow, clashing orange socks, pink trousers, a mauve tie and some flowery shirt. Randall had arrived from France with no suitcase, wearing après-ski boots (his shoes had worn out), an open-necked white shirt and a pair of mustard yellow trousers. The rest of his stuff he had left behind, crammed into a cupboard in someone's kitchen. He cheerfully told me that it was too dirty to bring home. And so, unable to change his clothes, he hit on a daring idea and left his wiry hair uncombed.

We walked towards the river along a wide avenue. Several cars passed us, and other legal guests, dressed in rather smart clothes, were on foot. The sky was clear and the stars did their usual bit. It was only just after nine. ' We'll never get in,' Nadine whispered as we came in view of the gangplank that led to a brightly lit boat. A couple of young men slouched on the gang-plank railings, scarves loosely hanging round their necks, watching newcomers suspiciously. One had a list in his hand, but he seemed rather embarrassed. Andrew nodded, and each of us who followed muttered 'good evening' and we were on the forbidden boat.

It was a drab party. Revolting coloured water passed off as wine stood in glasses on a table. Bowls of bananas and grapes were the only food. But the clothes were an even greater disappointment. A boy in shorts, a girl in a gym slip with green coloured tights, this was Oxford permissiveness. Behaviour was genteel. People ate bananas and grapes, drank and talked, and danced decorously. Robin Day, well known on British television for his exacting interviews, muttered, ' No one told me this was meant to be a permissive party.' He was not wearing his bow tie, just a dull flat kipper tie, and a dark suit. His very pretty wife Cathleen, was dressed in the usual mini-mini and felt quite Victorian. The guest of honour looked less permissive than anyone and rather cross.

' Must build up atmosphere ' was the order. Yet the atmosphere was artificial. Undergraduates evaluated each other in their degree capacity. 'Meet Potential First', or ' have you met Second?' or 'here is Third, but he's charming all the same'. Abstruse films and plays, erudite quotations, original judgements, *bons mots*, and the latest in wit floated through the self-conscious air. It was exhausting and I was delighted when the television cameras boarded the boat. Conversation rattled on, girls touched up their hair and looked languishingly into the lenses dreaming of a breakthrough into films. Two people were thrown in, when the lighting was right, and the camera man ready. Another undergraduate stripped to his underpants; dancing was as wild as it always had been; Kenneth Tynan looked bored. An elderly dwarfish man tried to recapture wild university days. I heard a voice behind me, 'Would you consider baring your breasts for twenty-five pounds?' I shook my head. The man asked several girls in the room. Each smiled sweetly but said No. Conforming with the spirit of the party, we left at twelve.

The *Cherwell* the following week gave a gently accurate account of the evening. 'Alas, Oxford is not as debauched as it likes to think. At the inaugural orgy of the Oxford Universal Permissive society on St Catherine's barge, the satyrs achieved not satiety, and the nymphs mislaid their mania.' A rival and more ancient permissive society was cited as being more authentic. WOUPS (Women's Oxford University Pregnant Society) is planned ' as an outlet for the frustrations of Schoolswomen. Woups women meet and knit small woollen clothes to be given as prizes to whoever becomes pregnant . . .' the *Cherwell* reported. It also told of another new club, Sexual Partners Club, known affectionately as Nip and Kip.

The revolt in Paris had subsided. The occupation ended and examinations were fixed for September. In England interest in revolution declined as the long summer holidays began. For me, it went out with a fizzle in the most unusual surroundings. I had found a leaflet at LSE announcing a day-long discussion on revolutionary culture in a North London Theatre. It was irresistible. My friend Louisa, pretty and untroubled, agreed to come. I had persuaded her to make contact with her generation. She was an apprentice in revolt although she tried to hide the fact by dressing all in black. With her long blonde hair tied in bright red ribbons she looked a veteran. I, in my psychedelic raincoat felt a nervous novice.

The Unity Theatre was well advertised. Slogans in glaring colours surmounting angry, distorted faces glared from the brick wall of the drab houses of Goldington Street NW1. We pushed open a tin door and walked through a rubbish dump into the theatre. The stalls were quite full. I passed a few distracted hippies, two young women holding small babies, bearded men in spectacles, intense faces hidden in long hair and pale thin girls in thick black stockings. On the stage, huddled in intimate groups, men in their early twenties in jeans and loose shirts sat talking in low voices. The air was hot and smoky. Louisa and I sat in the front row and stared at the stage. An enormous wide-open mouth devoured the back of the *décor*; a lone tooth, four feet high, stood near the footlights. On the end of a foreshortened arm a hand of gigantic proportions stretched out towards us. Gulliver was about to grab the Lilliputians, I thought. While Louisa gaped I took out my leaflet and accosted a young man with tousled yellow hair and a thin brown moustache, a member of the Bradford School of Art. 'Excuse me,' I began timidly. 'I've come from the LSE . . . this discussion . . . what exactly does it mean,' and I read out the title for the debate, 'The Challenge of a Socialist Sub-culture in a Neo-Capitalist Society?' 'You don't want to believe everything you read do you?' came the reply.

I sank back into my seat. I turned to my neighbour. She had thick black hair and was very pretty, dressed in moccasins and an Indian jacket. She was a follower, she said, of the Cartoon Archetypical Slogan theatre. 'We've got to revolutionise the theatre. It's run by fascists like the Lord Chamberlain. Plays only support the consumer society, propagate the existing regime . . .' I muttered something about Osborne and Pinter. 'It's all rubbish,' she went on. 'Sugar lumps fed to the public.'

'And if they like it and are prepared to pay to see it?'

'The public don't know what they want. You see,' she said in a lower voice, 'they are unaware.'

'Of what?'

'Of what is good.'

'It's just your word against theirs,' Louisa burst out.

She shook her head. The young man leant forward. 'Any play that won't make money is suppressed.'

Louisa could contain herself no longer. 'It is an open market,' she insisted. 'The public judge because the public pay.'

'You're prematurely corrupted,' the young man retorted with disgust.

Around us the talk was of Vietnam and the procession of 20th July, not of cultural revolution. I approached the Agit-Prop (Agitation Propaganda) desk beneath the footlights. 'They're the force behind all this,' a man had told me, 'The egg heads of the movement. Sort of LSE.' A girl sat writing; her black hair was pulled tight across her head and she wore thick glasses. I read from a pamphlet, 'Agit Prop, a co-ordinating service of revolutionary movement . . .'

'Any specific services to offer?' she asked curtly.

'I'm waiting to be convinced,' I said. 'When does the debate begin?'

'What debate? We're all agreed.'

'On what?'

She looked at me suspiciously. 'Revolution. We've got to destroy this capitalist system. It's nothing but a dictatorship. Tories, Labour, they're fascists.'

'But if they are elected by a majority?'

'What's a majority? Majorities aren't always right. And anyway elections are meaningless. People don't know what they're doing.' Here she weighed her words. ' They are politically unaware.'

'Oh, not that again,' Louisa muttered, and once again she burst out, ' If I vote for a party because I want to see lower taxes so I can buy a television set, how am I so unaware?' she asked simply.

'You don't really want a telly. You only think you do. Outside pressures, you see.'

'Are you aware?' I asked. She nodded. 'We've escaped the pressures. We're untainted, and so we must fight and build a real democracy; make people realise their true needs.'

'I think your ideas are rather fascist,' I said suddenly.

'Me fascist . . . Of all the cheek . . . Bert, where's Bert? I have never been called a fascist. Me fascist!'

The meeting was adjourned. Louisa and I hurried towards the exit. Two young men were holding out hats. 'For the cause, help the revolution,' they chanted. 'I'm sorry,' I said to one. 'I'm a conscientious objector.'

Before they could answer we had passed into the rubbish dump but we turned the wrong way and when we finally got to the street one of the collectors was pacing the pavement. Beside him stood a group of hefty sculpture students. He saw me and glared furiously. 'Wus it you wot said conscientious objector? Was it? Was it?' 'Yes, it was,' I said as calmly as I could. 'Explain, go on explain. Just what did you mean? Explain.'

'You couldn't explain the cultural revolution to me. I shan't explain to you.'

'Why not? Explain, go on, explain.' His hefty friends looked on menacingly.

'I have to tell you,' I said sadly, 'that we are both deeply disappointed in you.'

The stunned silence broke into a stream of invective. As Louisa and I hurried to my flower-power Mini voices screamed in our ears, 'stupid slobs, fat cows . . .'

The year was over and everyone scattered. Kate went to Perugia where she took a three-month course in Italian (the University paid for part of the expense). Patsy went to Yorkshire; Ian to the beer cellars in Munich to become a bar tender. John got a job as a waiter on the coast, which gave him the chance to pick up some bikini-clad lovelies. Paul went on a tour of French medieval battlements and Ned hitch-hiked towards Persia. He took his novel and his girl-friend with him. Richard worked as a lumberjack, then ran a man's boutique in Canada. And I, well I spent the summer writing this book.

What is more it has no end. It could be beginning again now. with the new academic year. No one knows what will happen. In Germany Danny the Red has been given a six-month suspended sentence for violent behaviour. 'We are children of violence,' he warned the judge. In Italy demands for university reform have not been met and more rioting must follow. In France the atmosphere is very uneasy. I went to Paris briefly. The cobblestone roads have disappeared beneath several inches of tarmac. The examinations that should have taken place in June were postponed till November. A few examinations held in September were boycotted, others passed peacefully. The exact reforms are not yet known, but the reformed university may no longer depend on the Ministry of Education, and may have a greater degree of autonomy and of student participation at all levels. The new Minister of Education, Monsieur Faure, has the temporary support of most students. He is ' assez révolutionnaire '. Much will depend on his attitude to free political expression within the university. This is the major issue, and is likely to remain so.

In England the new academic year began with a general demand for representation on the Senate, the professorial board that discusses university finance and the appointment of professors. At Sussex this change has taken place. Few universities have the climate of Sussex where students and teachers are treated as one unit. In older universities I doubt whether representation on the Senate will be easily accepted, yet (if enough students in a university want to take on more responsibility they surely should be given it. Otherwise what is the point of being taught to think? I fail to see why it is so sacrilegious to suggest that students should have a say in who teaches and who does not. A teacher has a job like anyone else, and why should he be any less removable? It is up to him to interest and inform his students. If he bores them stiff he is not doing his job. And who better than the students can judge if he is a bore?)

Violence in English universities will almost certainly increase. The Paris riots are an inspiration to any revolutionary, and English activists lag a long way behind their European contemporaries. The RSSF, a maoist militant group is swotting up the basic lessons on timing and co-ordination among sympathisers throughout England. Practice makes perfect, so the revolutionary agenda for 1968-9 will be full. The only effective counterforce to violence is a movement on the part of moderates challenging militant minorities in union and political meetings. Much is talked about the 'rights' of moderates. If they want these rights they must be prepared to fight for them.)

I don't suppose we are as unusual as we like to think. Violence has classified us as a renegade generation, and the general public throughout Western Europe is our hostile enemy: neither a worrying nor a surprising development. It seems to me that every age has its drop-ins and drop-outs. If anything is new it is perhaps the growing sense of community in this technological world. But for myself and for many others, the strongest feeling is also the least original. We revel in being young, and despite the great British, Italian, French and German publics, we are going to have a riot.